AF227575

PRAISE FOR

COMPETITIVE KINDNESS

❝ *Competitive Kindness* delivers a powerful truth every leader needs to hear: you don't have to sacrifice decency to win. Rob Clark offers a practical framework for leading with high standards and deep humanity, showing how kindness, accountability, and excellence reinforce one another. This book is a timely and compelling guide for anyone serious about building cultures that perform, last, and elevate the people within them.❞

BRAD D. SMITH
President, Marshall University
former chairman and CEO, Intuit

❝ Rob Clark delivers a powerful message and reminder for all leaders regardless of industry. You can achieve competitive excellence while serving with dignity and respect. *Competitive Kindness* embraces heart-lead leadership and provides the framework to navigate. Winning matters, and how you serve your team is more important than ever.❞

JERAMIAH DICKEY
director of athletics, Boise State University

" True leadership is not measured solely by outcomes, but by how people are treated along the journey. In *Competitive Kindness*, Rob Clark delivers a timely and necessary reminder that pursuing excellence and leading with compassion are not mutually exclusive—they are inseparable. This book belongs on the desk of every leader navigating pressure, competition, and responsibility in today's world. "

DAN BUTTERLY
conference commissioner, The Big West

" Over the past thirty years in college athletics, Rob Clark is one of the most kind and respectable people I have ever had the privilege of working with. *Competitive Kindness* reflects the core values I witnessed in working with Rob: doing our best daily to win championships, while treating people with respect and building a family atmosphere. "

JOANNE BOWERS,
head gymnastics coach,
University of Washington and San Jose State University

" A basic leadership principle is that 'you get what you design for.' Rob has done a masterful job using research, examples, and best practices in showing why and how competitive kindness is the key differentiator in winning the right way. For leaders looking for 'what good looks like' and a 'playbook' on how to design and align those elements essential for creating a culture of competitive kindness, I highly recommend Rob's timely roadmap to winning the right way. "

PAUL GUSTAVSON
president, Organization Planning & Design, Inc.

DR. ROB CLARK

COMPETITIVE KINDNESS

HOW TO WIN THE RIGHT WAY

Published by Maison Vero
3002 Dow Avenue, Suite 112
Tustin, CA 92780

Copyright © 2026 by Rob Clark

Maison Vero is a professional publishing house that partners with rising authors to bring their thought leadership to the world. By respecting the copyright of an author's intellectual property, you enable Maison Vero and the author to continue publishing exceptional books for years to come. We thank you for supporting the author's copyright by purchasing an authorized edition of this book.

No amount of this book may be reproduced or stored in any format, nor may it be uploaded to any website, database, language-learning model, or other repository, retrieval, or artificial intelligence system without express permission. All rights reserved.

Inquiries may be directed to: Maison Vero, 3002 Dow Avenue, Suite 112, Tustin, CA 92780, or info@graymilleragency.com.

For information about special discounts for bulk purchases, please call (949) 333-4872 or email info@graymilleragency.com.

Maison Vero is a partner brand of The Gray + Miller Agency, a speaking, literary, and talent consortium.

For more information on the talent represented by The Gray + Miller Agency, or to bring any of our thought leaders to your organization or live event, please visit our website at graymilleragency.com

Cover Design: Zach Sharples
Book Design: Mike Elwell

Manufactured in the United States of America

Paperback 978-1-969508-39-4   E-book 978-1-969508-40-0
Hardcover 978-1-969508-38-7

DEDICATION

To Emily, the greatest blessing in my life, whose example of
Competitive Kindness inspires me every day.

To Annie, Kate, and McCoy—there is greatness in each of you
that the world needs as you unleash your Competitive Kindness.

To Dede and Bobby who inspire me to push forward with
education and lift daily with faith.

To the mentors and leaders that show me how to win the right way.

For Him, who is the ultimate source of Competitive Kindness
and source of all that I hope to become.

CONTENTS

FOREWORD

BY COACH ALONZO CARTER

HEAD COACH, SACRAMENTO STATE FOOTBALL

Look, I believe in more than winning football games. We're going to compete at the highest level, prepare like champions, and demand results every Saturday.

But success has never been just about the scoreboard, you feel me?

I'm from West Oakland. Nothing in my life has come easy. It was rough. I had financial struggles, no father around, tough circumstances that could've taken me down a completely different path. But my mother? She made sure education was the way out. She pushed me when everything and almost everyone around me said give up. Education saved my life. Changed my trajectory. That's why I believe with everything in me that our success is measured by our players earning degrees and leaving prepared for life—not just Saturdays.

Coach Deon Sanders taught me to "dream while woke." Man, that hits different. It means living out your dreams with intention right now. It means being present, embracing what you're building, and showing love to every single person who helped you get there. My mother. My family. My community. They're all part of this dream.

That's what I believe. That's my coaching philosophy. And that's what my friend, Rob Clark, calls "Competitive Kindness" in this book.

You coach hard and care harder. You demand excellence, hold people accountable but invest in who they're becoming as men. Teach pride on and off the field. You teach how to represent family and community with integrity.

That's why our Beyond Football initiative shows kids in our community what's possible. By connecting with our community, reading to kids, and genuinely serving in the community we make an impact. Championships matter—but changing lives? That lasts forever.

I believe in building something that endures—rooted in education, service, toughness, and trust.

When you give and when you serve, you don't just win games. You win in life.

And Competitive Kindness opens your eyes to this, too!

Competitive Kindness is the leadership ethos
where teams maximize their potential to win
championships because every individual is
valued, **supported**, and **empowered**
to reach their full potential.

CHAPTER 1

THE MYTH THAT'S COSTING US EVERYTHING

In a world saturated with toxic hustle culture and performative leadership, Competitive Kindness emerges as the ultimate advantage—proving that winning and decency are not opposites, but powerful partners.

"You don't have to choose between being kind and being competitive. The best leaders are both."

There are clichés that I've heard my entire career—whispered in locker rooms, shouted across boardrooms, and passed down like absolute truth from one generation of leaders to the next.

It goes something like this:

If you want to win, you must be willing to break people.

Nice guys finish last.

Kindness is just another word for soft.

Show kindness, and you'll get eaten alive.

Only the ruthless survive.

I've watched this narrative shape everything from Fortune 500 company executives to athletic teams. I've seen leaders adopt personas that would make their own mothers cringe, all in the name of "whatever it takes to win." We've celebrated the screaming coaches, the ruthless CEOs, cutthroat colleagues, and the leaders who pride themselves on being the toughest person in the room. We've made heroes out of Competitive Cruelty.

And in doing so, we've quietly convinced ourselves that empathy, humility, and grace are luxuries we can't afford if we want to win.

But here's what I've discovered after decades of working alongside some of the most successful leaders in athletics and business: *That story is a lie. And it's costing us everything.*

THE TRUTH THAT CHANGES EVERYTHING

Competitive Kindness isn't the enemy of winning—it's the secret weapon. Competitive Kindness doesn't just build character; it builds champions. It's not just empowering; it's the ultimate competitive advantage. Competitive Kindness is fierce and gentle, demanding and dignified, all at once.

Let me be crystal clear about what I mean by Competitive Kindness, because this isn't some feel-good philosophy that sounds nice on a motivational poster.

WHAT COMPETITIVE KINDNESS REALLY MEANS

I get it—you hear the words "competitive" and "kindness" being lumped together, and that feels like a contradiction. You're right. You've probably also heard that tired old saying: "It doesn't matter who wins or loses, it's how you play the game." Rather than creating an excuse not to win, Competitive Kindness embraces the contradiction. Competitive Kindness is all about: "It matters who wins or loses AND it matters how you play the game."

Competitive Kindness is the leadership ethos of relentlessly pursuing peak accomplishments while treating people with unwavering dignity and respect. It's about helping both organizations and individuals reach their maximum potential simultaneously. It's the radical idea that you don't have to choose between winning and being decent—you can, and should, do both.

Competitive Kindness isn't about lowering standards or softening expectations. It doesn't compromise on excellence; it amplifies it. It's about choosing to lead with intention, creating cultures where people don't just perform, they flourish.

WHAT I'VE LEARNED IN THE ARENA

In my career in intercollegiate athletics administration, I've had a front-row seat to every type of leader you can imagine. From the administrative side, I've watched brilliant strategists and elite competitors who could dissect budgets and game films with equal precision, navigate complex university politics and motivate teams to achieve the impossible. I've also observed egotistical leaders who treated staff, coaches, and student athletes like chess pieces, caring only about their own personal brand while leaving a trail of broken relationships in their wake.

And then some fell somewhere in between—good people trying to balance results with relationships, often feeling they had to choose one or the other.

But here's what struck me most from my vantage point in athletics administration: the leaders who left the most profound impact—athletic directors whose departments didn't just win championships but built sustainable excellence, coaches whose teams didn't just perform but created lasting cultures, administrators whose staff members didn't just do their jobs but remained fiercely loyal—weren't just demanding. They were decent.

They remembered names and looked you in the eye during conversations. They made time for people when their calendars said they didn't have any. They corrected mistakes with clarity and coached with genuine care. They set impossibly high standards and then provided support to help people reach them.

That's Competitive Kindness in action. It's not performative or transactional. It's not fragile. It's fierce, it's intentional, and frankly, it's rare.

THE WORLD IS DESPERATE FOR A DIFFERENT WAY

We're living in an era of toxic hustle culture, where people wear burnout like a badge of honor. We're surrounded by political polarization that's seeped into our workplaces, social media feeds, and communities. We're drowning in performative leadership—people who talk a good game about culture and values but abandon those values the moment the pressure mounts or when it benefits them personally.

Meanwhile, organizations everywhere are struggling with the same challenges: attracting top talent, keeping good people, and building something that lasts beyond the current leadership. They're discovering that culture isn't just a buzzword—it's their brand. And you can't make a lasting culture with fear and ego. You build it with clarity, conviction, and compassion.

You build it with Competitive Kindness.

WHY THIS BOOK EXISTS

I didn't set out to write a book about kindness. I started trying to understand what makes championship teams and magnetic cultures. What makes some organizations pipelines of excellence while others implode under pressure? What separates leaders who inspire fierce loyalty from those who only command compliance?

Throughout my career in athletics administration, I've observed university presidents and administrators, athletic directors, coaches, and team captains, donors who are CEOs or owners of significant businesses, and a wide array of staff members throughout the university ecosystem. Different roles, different pressures, but the same pattern emerged every single time:

The best leaders don't sacrifice kindness for competitiveness. They integrate the two through Competitive Kindness.

They set the bar incredibly high and then guide others to reach it. They correct with empathy and inspire through example. They build trust over time, not just results on a scoreboard. And they win—not just championships, but the hearts and minds of the people they lead.

WHAT'S COMING NEXT

In the chapters ahead, we'll explore what Competitive Kindness looks like in practice. I'll share stories from locker rooms, startups, and Fortune 500 companies. We'll examine how to make Competitive Kindness a core part of your culture without compromising your standards. You'll meet coaches, executives, and professionals who are proving every day that Competitive Kindness doesn't just work—it wins.

We'll also dive into the specific practices and habits that help you lead with Competitive Kindness in high-performance environments, because Competitive Kindness isn't just a mindset—it's a leadership style that can be learned.

THE QUESTION THAT STARTED IT ALL

But before we go any further, I want you to ask yourself this question: who told you that you had to choose between winning and kindness? Was it a coach who screamed at you until you performed? Was it the boss who believed fear was the most effective motivator? Was it a work culture or sports team that celebrated the loudest, toughest, most ruthless person in the room? Was it a prospective employer that mistook arrogance for confidence?

Because here's what I've discovered: the most competitive people I know aren't cold or cruel. They're kind. They ALSO happen to be relentless in their pursuit of excellence.

And that's precisely the kind of leader the world is hungry for right now.

WHEN COMPETITIVE KINDNESS CHANGED EVERYTHING

Leaders who honor people's humanity while demanding
excellence create sustainable success,
as valued employees exceed expectations through
commitment rather than compliance.

"Real leadership starts when you honor what matters most to others."

It was a sweltering Los Angeles afternoon, the kind where the smog hangs heavy and the sun beats down mercilessly on the football field. Cleats are pounding turf, coaches are barking instructions, and the unrelenting grind of two-a-day practices is wearing everyone thin. Another Sunday at fall camp, right?

Except for me, it wasn't just another Sunday. And that was the problem.

THE MOMENT THAT CHANGED MY UNDERSTANDING OF LEADERSHIP

While my body sprinted hard, my mind and heart stood motionless on that field. I felt completely off, not because of the heat, the exhaustion, or even the brutal practice schedule. It was because of what day it was—Sunday. A day I'd grown up treating as sacred. A day meant for worship, rest, and spiritual renewal. But here I was, suiting up for practice like it was any other day.

The internal conflict was eating me alive.

Here's the thing about being an underclassman on a college football team: you're constantly trying to prove yourself. You're fighting for playing time, fighting for respect, fighting to show you belong. The last thing you want to do is rock the boat or give anyone a reason to question your commitment. But I couldn't shake this conviction burning inside me. I knew I wasn't playing my best because I wasn't being true to who I am at my core.

So, I made what felt like the riskiest decision of my young athletic career. I walked into my head coach's office.

I didn't storm in with demands or ultimatums. I came with honesty—and a promise.

"Coach Widolff," I said with my heart pounding, "I haven't been playing my best, and after some reflection, I believe it's because I haven't been true to my core beliefs. With your permission, would it be okay if I didn't practice on Sundays? I'll come in early Monday morning to catch up on film and lift before anyone else arrives. I'll work twice as hard every other day of the week. I just… I need that day."

I held my breath, waiting for the explosion. Waiting to be told I was soft, uncommitted, not cut out for this level of competition. Instead, my coach looked at me—not with frustration or confusion, but with something I didn't expect: *Competitive Kindness.*

Then he said something that has shaped my leadership philosophy ever since:

"Thank you for having the courage to stand up for who you are. We need that type of leadership on this team right now. Let's work together on a plan that builds the team and helps you become the best player you can be for us."

The look on my face must have been priceless. Coach continued:

"You're not alone on this team. Others on this team will follow you. Keep leading like this and we will win some ballgames!"

COMPETITIVE KINDNESS IN ACTION

That response wasn't just about accommodating one player's request. It was Competitive Kindness in its purest form.

My coach easily could have shut me down. He could have questioned my dedication, benched me, kicked me off the team, or made an example out of me to the rest of the team. Instead, he demonstrated something powerful: respecting a team member's values didn't make us less competitive—it made us stronger.

He understood that Competitive Kindness isn't about lowering standards or making exceptions that compromise excellence. It's about recognizing that when people can be authentic to who they are, they perform at levels you never thought possible.

THE TRANSFORMATION THAT FOLLOWED

What happened next still gives me chills when I think about it.

In the weeks that followed, something began to shift in our team culture. The program had been stuck in a deep losing streak, struggling to find our identity, playing like a collection of individuals rather than a unified team. But slowly, we began to find our rhythm. Purpose. Unity.

We started winning. Not just games, but something more valuable—trust, confidence, and respect for one another.

It didn't happen overnight, but it started with that single moment of Competitive Kindness. My coach had empowered one voice to be authentic, and soon, many others found the courage to do the same.

The years that followed became the most successful in Occidental College football history. We made a deep run in the NCAA playoffs, losing only to the eventual national champions, and achieved a Top 10 national ranking. But more importantly, Coach had built a culture rooted in Competitive Kindness and instilled it throughout the team's leadership.

THE LEADERSHIP LESSON
THAT CHANGED EVERYTHING

Here's what my coach may not have realized at that moment: he was teaching me one of the most profound leadership lessons I would ever learn.

Competitive Kindness starts when leaders make space for people to live their values—and still expect them to chase greatness.

In athletics, coaches are often judged solely by their win-loss records. But the truly exceptional ones—the ones who build lasting legacies—are remembered for how they treated people, especially when no one was watching. They understand that you can honor someone's humanity and still demand their excellence.

THE RIPPLE EFFECT OF
BEING SEEN, HEARD, AND VALUED

I've carried that lesson into every role I've held since—as an athletics administrator, as a team member, as a mentor. And I've witnessed firsthand what happens when people feel genuinely safe and seen in their environment.

They don't just comply with expectations—they exceed them. They don't just show up—they bring their whole selves. They don't just perform—they transform.

That's the power of Competitive Kindness. It doesn't just unlock potential; it unleashes it. It doesn't just build compliance; it breeds deep, lasting commitment. It changes the entire dynamic from "do what I say because I'm in charge" to "be who you are—and give everything you've got because we believe in you and will help you become your best."

WHAT HAPPENS WHEN YOU BUILD ON THAT FOUNDATION

When you build a team, an organization, or a culture on the foundation of Competitive Kindness, something remarkable happens. People stop holding back. They stop playing it safe. They stop hiding parts of themselves because they're afraid people won't accept them.

Instead, they lean in. They take risks. They bring their full creativity, passion, and energy to the pursuit of excellence.

And when that happens? Watch what unfolds.

The results speak for themselves—not just in wins and losses, but in the quality of relationships, the depth of trust, and the sustainability of success. Because Competitive Kindness doesn't just help you win games; it enables you to build something that lasts long after the final whistle blows.

That's the kind of leadership the world is hungry for. And it all started with a coach who understood that being kind and being competitive aren't opposites—they're the perfect combination.

COMPETITIVE KINDNESS IS MORE THAN BEING NICE

Great leaders know not to confuse being nice with being kind. They are distinctly different and when you combine direct accountability with genuine support, you get real results.

"Kindness is not weakness. It's a strength wrapped in humility and wielded with fierce purpose." — The Program

There's a conversation that has happened hundreds of times in my career in athletics administration, and it usually starts the same way. A coach, administrator, or team leader will pull me aside and say something like, "I want to lead this team to championship success, but my players (or staff members) are too soft. How do I push them to be champions without me having to be so soft and nice?"

And that's when I know we need to have a deeper conversation. Because the word "nice" is killing our leadership potential.

THE GREAT MISCONCEPTION
THAT'S HOLDING US BACK

Let's be crystal clear about something: Competitive Kindness *isn't just being nice.* I cannot make a more crucial distinction.

Too often, kindness in leadership gets confused with agreeableness, softness, and a tendency to avoid conflict. People think kindness means sugarcoating hard truths, avoiding accountability, or placating others to prevent discomfort. Nothing could be further from the truth.

Competitive Kindness is an intentional blend of grit and grace, rooted in high performance standards, personal accountability, and deep respect for others. It's a powerful force that drives exceptional performance by balancing genuine human connection with uncompromising excellence. But at its core, Competitive Kindness builds people and organizations to reach their maximum potential for the benefit of all because it's the right thing to do.

Let me show you what I mean with a story that plays out on fields and in offices every single day.

THE TALE OF TWO TEAMMATES

Let's imagine that you are on a football team. Your teammate keeps missing the same critical block on the football field. Play after play, the offensive strategy crumbles because of this one missed assignment. The team can't move the ball; drives stall out and games slip away.

Now, here's how this unfolds:

The "nice" teammate offers gentle encouragement: "Hang in there! You'll get them next time." It sounds supportive. But here's what really happens: the mistake goes uncorrected, the play continues to fail, the team doesn't score, the team loses the game, and the player gets benched. He never reaches his athletic potential and his confidence is crushed, which affects many other facets of his personal life. Everyone loses. Mission failed.

The teammate practicing Competitive Kindness takes an entirely different approach: "Hey! Your assignment is to block the linebacker this way. Without you executing that block, we can't make this play work. You've got this!"

Notice the difference? It might feel uncomfortable to address the issue directly, but that's precisely what Competitive Kindness demands. Because here's the truth: we need to win games to become champions. We need to score points to win games. And we need that block to be made so we can move the ball and achieve our goals.

Additionally, that player missing the block has a lot riding on his success, including a scholarship or other financial compensation, potential career implications, and his mental health and well-being, among many other elements in his life. He needs that correction as much as the team needs his assignment fulfilled. Leading with Competitive Kindness corrects so that the player and the team will thrive.

That's Competitive Kindness in action. You can be more than just pleasant by doing the truly kind thing: helping someone succeed rather than watching them fail repeatedly.

TAKING THE NEXT STEP FROM PREVIOUS STUDIES

Several authors and scholars have posited that effective leadership requires more than simply being nice—it requires kindness. Being nice often shuns the discomfort that accountability brings. Eric Kapitulik, a former Marine Corps special operations officer and founder of *The Program*, shared a model of high-performance teams that function through shared adversity, radical honesty, and deep commitment. Kapitulik's teams endured grueling training experiences—shared suffering that reveals character and forges trust. But what's most revealing isn't just who survives. It's those who *serve* others during suffering. The best teammates lift others even when they're struggling themselves. These are elements of Competitive Kindness: empathy under pressure, service without spotlight, loyalty without condition. He said:

"Kindness is not weakness. It's a strength wrapped in humility and wielded with fierce purpose." — *The Program*

Competitive Kindness builds upon Kapitulik's fierce mission-driven purpose, which is dual in nature: winning for the organization and building people into the best versions of themselves.

Organizational psychology scholars developed a theory of compassionate accountability in the workplace. It is a leadership style that combines care with candor (Boyatzis, Smith & Blaize, 2006). Compassionate accountability does not let people off the hook through niceties. Instead, it calls them *up* to a higher standard through encouragement, feedback, and discipline. It is a method of communication that holds people accountable to a standard for performative success.

Competitive Kindness goes one step further than compassionate accountability—leaders hold their people accountable not only to meet the organization's goals, but also to genuinely desire their people to become the best versions of themselves. That genuine approach of Competitive Kindness is rooted in love.

Psychologists Greg Walton and Geoffrey Cohen have conducted fascinating studies on what they call "wise feedback." They discovered that when leaders combine high expectations with genuine expressions of belief in an individual's potential, performance and motivation increase dramatically—especially among people who are struggling or underrepresented. The message is clear: *people rise when they feel seen and believed in.*

Competitive Kindness goes one step further than "wise feedback"—leaders must care more about the people they lead than simply reaching their performance potential at work. While that will be a byproduct of Competitive Kindness, Competitive Kindness says: "I believe in who we can become and, because I do, I won't let you settle for being less than you can become."

Competitive Kindness builds on the ideas that kindness is not the same as niceness, and incorporates concepts such as compassionate accountability and wise feedback, while embracing the uncomfortable truth that leaders are responsible for the overall well-being of those they lead. Kind competitors seek the best in others while expecting the best from themselves. They offer correction, not criticism. With Competitive Kindness, people can grow to reach their potential—and we will insist that they do.

It's not about being "nice." It's about being real, being committed, and being all in—for both the people and the mission. It's about becoming a champion—in the truest, strictest, most transformational sense of the word.

And that's the kind of leader the world desperately needs.

CHAPTER 4

THE HIDDEN PRICE OF COMPETITIVE CRUELTY

The profound irony of leadership today is that the cruel behaviors leaders think make them competitive actually undermine their competitiveness—but at what cost?

"Distrust all in whom the impulse to punish is powerful."
Nietzsche, *Thus Spoke Zarathustra*

"You can drive others through fear for a time—but eventually, that same fear will consume you too."

In the relentless pursuit of competitive advantage, some leaders make a fateful choice: they embrace Competitive Cruelty—the deliberate use of harshness, manipulation, and fear as strategic tools to achieve results. They convince themselves that kindness is weakness, that compassion is compromise, and that only the ruthless rise to the top.

This chapter exposes the devastating truth behind this philosophy. While Competitive Cruelty may deliver short-term gains, it exacts a price that few leaders anticipate and fewer still can afford to pay. They not only measure the cost in damaged relationships or toxic cultures, though these consequences are severe. The heaviest toll falls on the leaders themselves, manifesting in physical, emotional, mental, and spiritual ways.

When we choose Competitive Cruelty over Competitive Kindness, we don't just harm others. We systematically destroy ourselves.

THE ANATOMY OF COMPETITIVE CRUELTY

Competitive Cruelty isn't simply bad leadership—it's a deliberate mindset that views harshness as a competitive advantage. Leaders who embrace this approach believe that:

- Fear motivates better than inspiration
- Control produces better results than collaboration
- Criticism drives improvement faster than encouragement
- Dominance creates respect more effectively than service
- Winning justifies any means necessary

Unlike incompetent leadership, which often stems from a lack of skill or awareness, Competitive Cruelty is intentional. These leaders, who have chosen to weaponize their authority, view relationships as transactions and people as resources to be exploited for maximum output. Most often, the output is success, which can drive additional power, money, an enhanced personal brand, or any other form of self-aggrandizement.

The irony is profound. By pursuing competitive advantage through cruelty, these leaders ultimately undermine their own competitiveness in ways they never anticipated.

THE FOUR-FOLD DESTRUCTION:
HOW COMPETITIVE CRUELTY CONSUMES ITS OWN

1. The Physical Reckoning: When the Body Rebels

The human body wasn't designed to sustain the chronic stress that Competitive Cruelty demands. Leading through fear, manipulation, and constant control creates a physiological feedback loop that gradually destroys the leader's health.

Research reveals this stark reality. A 2018 meta-analysis in *The Journal of Organizational Behavior* found that leaders who adopt authoritarian or abusive styles experience chronically elevated cortisol levels, the stress hormone that, when sustained, becomes toxic to every central body system. These leaders carry their stress home, their bodies unable to distinguish between the battlefield they've created at work and the rest of their lives.

The contrast is striking. Leaders who engage in supportive, kind behaviors report significantly lower rates of cardiovascular disease and sleep disruption, according to a 2021 study in the *Journal of Occupational Health Psychology*. The American Institute of Stress found that executives operating in high-pressure, low-compassion environments are twice as likely to experience stress-related illnesses, including hypertension and gastrointestinal disorders.

Competitive Cruelty doesn't just stress the leader's targets—it places the leader under siege by their own biology. The body keeps score, and the bill always comes due.

2. The Emotional Wasteland: The Death of Connection

No consequence of Competitive Cruelty is more tragic than emotional erosion. What begins as strategic detachment—the belief that "tough decisions require distance"—gradually becomes an inability to connect with others or even with oneself.

A 2020 study in *The Leadership Quarterly* documented this progression. Leaders who regularly suppress empathy and compassion don't just become less caring—they become emotionally numb. Over time, they lose access to the full spectrum of human emotion, reporting decreased job satisfaction and increased burnout as their capacity for joy, wonder, and genuine connection atrophies.

Research from Yale's Center for Emotional Intelligence shows that leaders who regularly engage in harsh behaviors experience higher rates of loneliness, irritability, and resentment. They become isolated, surrounded by people yet fundamentally alone, because they've taught others that vulnerability and authenticity are liabilities.

"Empathy fatigue" becomes self-induced. When kindness is systematically suppressed, emotions aren't processed—they're buried. The result is leaders who appear strong on the surface but are hollowing out from within, their emotional range reduced to variations of anger, frustration, and cynical detachment.

Meanwhile, leaders who practice Competitive Kindness develop greater emotional resilience. They remain connected to the full range of human experience, drawing strength from authentic relationships and finding themselves supported when pressure mounts.

3. The Mental Deterioration: The Cognitive Cost of Cruelty

Competitive Cruelty's assault on mental faculties is perhaps its most counterintuitive consequence. Leaders who embrace this approach often believe they're being more rational, more strategic, and more mentally tough. The research tells a different story.

A landmark study published in the *Academy of Management Journal* (2019) found that leaders who routinely use fear-based motivation experience cognitive overload. The mental energy required to maintain control, manage threats, and suppress empathy leaves fewer resources for higher-order thinking. The result: poorer decision-making, increased impulsivity, and reduced creativity—the very qualities these leaders need most.

Competitive Cruelty also leads to moral disengagement, a psychological phenomenon where individuals rationalize unethical behavior to reduce internal conflict. A 2022 study in the *Journal of Business Ethics* found that leaders who abandon kindness gradually compromise their moral compass, making increasingly questionable decisions that damage their reputations and, in extreme cases, lead to legal consequences.

The mental clarity these leaders seek through dominance remains elusive. True cognitive excellence emerges from integrity and inner alignment—qualities that Competitive Cruelty systematically destroys.

4. The Spiritual Drought: Losing the Why

Every leader begins with purpose—a deeper motivation beyond profits and prestige. But Competitive Cruelty has a peculiar way of disconnecting leaders from their original inspiration. As they prioritize winning at all costs, they lose sight of why winning mattered to them in the first place.

A 2021 study in *Work, Employment and Society* identified this phenomenon as "existential stress"—a sense of purposelessness and internal conflict that emerges when leaders' actions consistently contradict their deeper values. Harvard's Human Flourishing Program found that leaders who suppress relational virtues like kindness, humility, and forgiveness are significantly more likely to experience anxiety, cynicism, and depression.

This spiritual erosion doesn't happen overnight. It's gradual, almost imperceptible. But the cumulative effect is devastating, as leaders find themselves successful by external measures yet fundamentally empty. Even when they've achieved their goals, they have lost their souls.

A TOXIC TITAN'S RISE AND FALL

The corporate landscape is littered with examples of Competitive Cruelty's ultimate futility. Consider Uber under Travis Kalanick's leadership before 2017. While the company experienced meteoric growth, internal investigations revealed a culture built on fear, aggression, and unchecked power.

Kalanick, once praised for his brilliance and drive, became the embodiment of Competitive Cruelty's promise and peril. His approach delivered rapid results—and ultimately destroyed him. Plagued by scandals, lawsuits, and a complete collapse of his reputation, he was forced from the company he built.

According to *MIT Sloan Management Review*, toxic leaders often "burn the candle at both ends," thereby accelerating short-term results while simultaneously destroying culture and themselves. The tragedy wasn't just what Kalanick lost, but what he could have sustained had he chosen Competitive Kindness alongside competitive drive.

THE ORGANIZATIONAL CARNAGE: HOW COMPETITIVE CRUELTY SPREADS

The damage extends far beyond the cruel leader. Like a virus, Competitive Cruelty spreads throughout organizations, creating systems that are simultaneously high-performing and self-destructing. When leaders abandon core virtues, the effects cascade:

- Empathy abandoned leads to higher employee turnover as people flee toxic environments
- Patience discarded results in increased workplace conflict and communication breakdown
- Integrity compromised causes loss of public trust and stakeholder confidence
- Support withdrawn creates psychological fear that kills innovation and risk-taking

A 2023 Gallup poll revealed that employees who perceive their leader as harsh are six times more likely to be disengaged and three times more likely to seek outside employment within six months. The competitive advantage that cruelty promises becomes a competitive disadvantage as talent flees, innovation stagnates, and reputation suffers.

THE PATH BACK: COMPETITIVE KINDNESS AS REDEMPTION

The good news embedded in this sobering analysis is that these outcomes aren't inevitable. Leaders can change courses, and many do. The research on leadership transformation is as compelling as the research on leadership destruction.

Practicing daily gratitude and empathy literally rewires the brain for connection, according to UC Berkeley's Greater Good Science Center. Rebuilding relationships through active listening and acknowledgment of past harm restores credibility and trust, as documented in the *Journal of Applied Behavioral Science* (2020).

Most importantly, re-aligning leadership with purpose, values, and Competitive Kindness doesn't just heal the leader—it transforms entire organizational trajectories. Teams that experience this transition often describe it as organizational resurrection, with energy, creativity, and performance returning to levels that exceeded even the cruel leader's previous "successful" periods.

THE ULTIMATE COMPETITION FOR YOU: CRUELTY VS. KINDNESS

In the end, Competitive Cruelty and Competitive Kindness represent two fundamentally different approaches to the same challenge: achieving sustainable excellence while leading others.

Competitive Cruelty promises quick results through dominance but delivers long-term destruction through disconnection. It's a strategy that consumes its own foundation, ultimately defeating itself through the very means it uses to achieve victory.

Competitive Kindness offers a different path—one that recognizes kindness not as weakness but as the ultimate competitive advantage. It builds sustainable excellence through connection, creates results that endure because they're founded on trust, and develops leaders who grow stronger rather than more brittle under pressure.

The choice between these approaches isn't just a leadership decision—it's a life decision. Because how we lead others inevitably becomes how we experience our own existence.

As Desmond Tutu observed:

"There is nothing wrong with having power. What matters is how you use it."

The leaders who understand this truth don't just win; they win big. They flourish. And they create organizations where others can thrive alongside them.

The myth of the highly successful competitively cruel leader—stoic, detached, unkind—is not only false, but also fatal. It leads to burnout, physical and relational decay, poor performance, and spiritual drought. Competitive Kindness is the antidote. Not just for your team. Not just for your organization. But for your soul.

THE TRANSFORMATIONAL POWER OF COMPETITIVE KINDNESS ON INDIVIDUALS AND ORGANIZATIONS

Kindness enhances performance—creating measurable competitive advantages in decision-making, team effectiveness, innovation, and financial results.

"Responsibilities gravitate to the man who can shoulder them; power flows to the man who knows how."
Elbert Hubbard

Here's what everyone gets wrong about kindness: while other leaders play "tough," the kind ones are quietly crushing the competition with sharper decisions, higher-performing teams, and profit margins that don't lie. Figuratively killing Competitive Cruelty with kindness.

I have spent years in boardrooms where "nice guys finish last" was treated like the absolute truth. In these spaces, cockiness is celebrated as confidence, and cruelty is akin to toughness. You know the drill—drive hard, demand more, and kindness is something you save for the company holiday party. But here's what the research overwhelmingly confirms: we've been getting it backwards.

The most compelling evidence from psychology, neuroscience, and organizational behavior shows that kindness isn't the opposite of competitive excellence—it's actually the secret sauce that makes it sustainable. When I talk about kindness, I'm not suggesting we lower our standards or go soft on performance. I'm talking about a research-backed approach that integrates genuine care for people with a relentless pursuit of results. And the data? It's absolutely game changing.

WHAT HAPPENS IN YOUR BRAIN WHEN YOU LEAD WITH KINDNESS

Here's something that blew me away when I first learned about it: being kind literally rewires your brain for better performance. I'm not talking feel-good platitudes here. I'm talking complex neuroscience that should make any performance-focused leader sit up and take notice.

The Neuroscience Revolution in Leadership

When researchers at Stanford put compassionate leaders through brain imaging studies, they discovered something remarkable: kindness triggers a cascade of neurochemical changes that essentially optimize your brain for high performance. Think of it as upgrading your mental operating system.

According to Lutz et al., here's what happens in your brain when you consistently lead with kindness and compassion:

YOUR PREFRONTAL CORTEX GETS STRONGER: This is your brain's CEO—the part responsible for executive decision-making, strategic thinking, and emotional regulation. Brain scans show that compassionate leaders have measurably more vigorous activity in this region (Lutz et al., 2004). What does this mean for you? Better judgment calls, clearer thinking under pressure, and the ability to see the bigger picture when everyone else is getting lost in the weeds.

YOUR AMYGDALA CALMS DOWN: The amygdala is essentially your brain's alarm system, it triggers fight-or-flight responses. When you practice compassionate leadership, this region becomes less reactive (Lutz et al., 2004). Practically speaking, this means you're less likely to make knee-jerk decisions when things get tough, and you can stay calm and focused when everyone around you is panicking.

YOUR ANTERIOR CINGULATE CORTEX LIGHTS UP: This is your brain's empathy center, and it's also heavily involved in attention and conflict monitoring. When this region is more active, you become better at reading situations, understanding what your team needs, and spotting problems before they become crises.

THE CHEMICAL COCKTAIL OF HIGH PERFORMANCE

Now, here's where it gets fascinating—the neurochemical changes. When you lead with genuine kindness and compassion, your brain starts producing what I call "the performance cocktail:"

OXYTOCIN SURGES: Often called the "bonding hormone," oxytocin doesn't just make you feel good—it literally enhances your ability to trust, collaborate, and build strong relationships. For leaders, this translates to stronger team cohesion and better stakeholder relationships. The Stanford research showed 47 percent increases in oxytocin levels among compassionate leaders (Seppälä et al., 2017).

CORTISOL DROPS DRAMATICALLY: Cortisol is your stress hormone, and while a bit of stress can be motivating, chronic high cortisol levels are performance killers. They impair memory, reduce creative thinking, and weaken your immune system. Compassionate leaders exhibit 23 percent lower cortisol levels, indicating they maintain peak cognitive performance even during high-stress periods (Seppälä et al., 2017).

DOPAMINE AND SEROTONIN INCREASE: These are your brain's reward and mood-regulation chemicals. Higher levels mean better motivation, improved mood stability, and enhanced learning ability. When you're kind to others, your brain rewards you with these performance-enhancing chemicals.

THE MIRROR NEURON EFFECT

Let's take this up another level. Studies also show that your brain changes don't just affect you—they affect everyone around you. Mirror neurons are specialized brain cells that fire both when you act and when you observe someone else performing that action (Porges, 2011). When your team sees you operating from a place of calm and competitively kind leadership, their mirror neurons start firing in similar patterns.

Essentially, your neurochemical state becomes contagious. When you're operating with that optimized brain chemistry—low stress, high focus, strong emotional regulation—your team's brains start mimicking those patterns. It's like you're upgrading their neural operating system just by how you show up as a leader.

REAL-WORLD BRAIN PERFORMANCE

Let me give you a practical example of how this plays out. Imagine you're in a high-stakes meeting where tensions are running high, deadlines are looming, and everyone's stress levels are through the roof.

The leader using Competitive Cruelty might respond with greater pressure, more demands, and greater urgency. But here's what happens in their brain: cortisol spikes, the amygdala goes into overdrive, and the prefrontal cortex—that crucial decision-making center—actually goes offline. They might achieve immediate compliance, but the decisions made in this state are often poor.

Now imagine a leader who has trained their brain through Competitive Kindness. Their prefrontal cortex stays online, their cortisol remains manageable, and they can access their full cognitive capacity. They might take a breath, acknowledge the stress everyone's feeling, and then guide the team toward solutions rather than just adding more pressure. Not only do they make better decisions, but their calm, focused energy also helps regulate everyone else's nervous systems.

THE NEUROPLASTICITY ADVANTAGE

The most exciting part of these studies supporting Competitive Kindness is the long-term impact. These brain changes compound over time. Neuroplasticity research shows that the more you practice compassion in leadership, the stronger these neural pathways become (Jazaieri et al., 2013). It's like building muscle—the more you work out your compassion circuits, the more naturally they fire. In other words, your brain literally rewires itself to become more effective.

Leaders who have been practicing Competitive Kindness for years show dramatically different brain patterns than those who haven't. Their brains are literally wired for better performance, better relationships, and better decision-making. They don't have to work as hard to stay calm under pressure or to read complex social situations—their brains have been optimized for these leadership challenges.

YOUR BODY ACTUALLY GETS STRONGER WHEN YOU'RE KIND

When Stanford's researchers studied compassionate leaders, they found something remarkable. Compassionate leaders had 23 percent lower cortisol (that's your stress hormone) and 47 percent higher oxytocin (the "love hormone"). What does this mean for you as a leader? Your body literally operates better. You think more clearly under pressure, you recover faster from stressful situations, and—here's the kicker—your team picks up on this energy and starts performing better too.

Let's add to the fun. The Institute of HeartMath's research found that leaders who approach challenges with genuine care and appreciation have measurably better heart rate variability—which is basically your body's ability to handle stress and bounce back. We're talking about

18 percent lower inflammation markers, which means you're less likely to get sick and more likely to maintain your energy during those crucial high-pressure periods.

WHY KIND LEADERS MAKE BETTER DECISIONS (AND HANDLE PRESSURE LIKE PROS)

How can you better handle the pressure to win championships in your work? Daniel Goleman's team studied over 500 senior executives and found that the leaders who scored highest on compassion were also the ones who made the best decisions under pressure—in fact, 40 percent better performance on complex challenges (Goleman, Boyatzis, & McKee, 2013). Think about what this means in your day-to-day leadership. When you're facing a crisis, when the stakes are high, when everyone's looking to you for answers, and when your brain needs to be firing on all cylinders, it is the kindest leaders who are the ones whose brains actually work best.

BOUNCING BACK FASTER THAN EVER

What about adapting to change or recovering from past failures? The University of Pennsylvania scholars found that compassionate leaders recover from setbacks 34 percent faster and adapt to change 28 percent better than their more traditionally aggressive counterparts (Southwick & Charney, 2012). I've seen this play out countless times. The leaders who approach setbacks with curiosity rather than blame, who see failures as learning opportunities rather than reasons to punish—they're the ones who keep moving forward while others get stuck in the drama of blaming, complaining, and defensiveness. In today's world, where change is the only constant, this isn't just nice to have—it's essential for survival.

THE MAGIC OF PSYCHOLOGICAL SAFETY
(AND WHY YOUR TEAM'S BEST IDEAS ARE HIDING)

Google spent years trying to figure out what makes teams extraordinary. They called it *Project Aristotle*, and what they discovered will change how you think about team performance forever. It wasn't the most intelligent people, the most significant budgets, or the best strategies that made the difference. It was psychological safety—and guess what creates that? Competitive Kindness.

Teams with leaders who created safe, supportive environments performed 76 percent better and solved problems 47 percent more effectively (Rozovsky, 2015). And here's what really matters for you—these teams weren't just happier, they were dramatically more innovative and productive.

BUILDING REAL TRUST
(NOT JUST PROFESSIONAL COURTESY)

Harvard's Amy Edmondson has spent decades studying this, and her findings are clear: when leaders approach their teams with genuine care and respect, people aren't just nicer to each other—they actually perform better. We're talking about 67 percent more learning behavior and 47 percent fewer critical errors (Edmondson, 2019).

This research validates what many of us have suspected—when people feel genuinely cared for, they bring their whole selves to work. They ask the hard questions, they admit their mistakes before they become disasters, and they come up with solutions that blow everyone away.

WHAT HAPPENS WHEN
EVERYONE FEELS LIKE THEY BELONG

The inclusion research is compelling here. When leaders demonstrate genuine care and cultural humility (what researchers call inclusive leadership), their teams are 35 percent more likely to outperform others and 70 percent more likely to capture new markets (Catalyst, 2020). McKinsey's data shows these organizations are 33 percent more profitable (McKinsey & Company, 2020). But beyond the numbers, think about what this means for your culture. When everyone feels valued and heard, you're not just being nice—you're unleashing the hidden potential of Competitive Kindness.

THE BOTTOM LINE: HOW KINDNESS DRIVES BUSINESS RESULTS

Okay, let's talk numbers—because at the end of the day, we all answer to results, and the research here is compelling. Welcome to the competitive side of Competitive Kindness.

Your People Will Actually Want to Stay

Gallup's latest research shows something that should make every leader pay attention: employees who feel genuinely cared for by their managers are 3.8 times more likely to be engaged at work (Gallup, 2023). Organizations with compassionate leadership cultures see 40 percent lower turnover and 58 percent fewer safety incidents. Think about what turnover costs you, not just in recruiting and training, but in lost knowledge, disrupted relationships, and decreased morale. When people feel valued and cared for, they don't just stay longer; they give more of themselves to the work.

Innovation Thrives When People Feel Safe to Think Big

Here's research that should excite any leader who wants their team to innovate. Studies across 238 teams found that compassionate leadership increases creative performance by 42 percent (Liu et al., 2018). When you create an environment where people aren't afraid to fail, where they know you've got their back, that's when the breakthrough ideas start flowing. The Center for Creative Leadership found that teams led by empathetic leaders achieve 67 percent higher creative problem-solving and 34 percent higher innovation success rates (Van Velsor et al., 2010). In today's competitive landscape, that kind of creative advantage can be the difference between leading your market and watching others pass you by.

The Financial Impact Is Real

Organizations with compassionate leadership cultures show 21 percent higher profitability and 19 percent higher revenue growth over five years (Frost, 2003). The Wharton School found that companies led by compassionate leaders have 2.3 times the revenue growth of their competitors (Grant, 2013). Harvard Business Review's analysis of S&P 500 companies found that the most compassionate leaders outperformed the market by 147 percent and showed 35 percent greater employee productivity (George, 2003). These aren't feel-good statistics—these are competitive advantages that show up on your P&L.

WHY THIS MATTERS FOR THE LONG GAME

Here's what I find most compelling about Competitive Kindness: it's not just about short-term gains. The research shows that organizations built on compassionate leadership principles are simply more resilient and sustainable over time.

WEATHERING THE STORMS

When economic downturns hit, when markets shift, when crises emerge—that's when you really see the difference. Research spanning decades shows that companies with compassionate leadership cultures demonstrate 89 percent greater resilience during tough times and recover 67 percent faster from crises (Dutton et al., 2006).

I've watched organizations go through layoffs, the impacts of COVID, market crashes, and industry disruptions. The ones who maintain their humanity, who continue to care for their people even during difficult decisions, they're the ones who come out stronger. Their people rally around them, their customers stay loyal, and their recovery is faster.

BUILDING LEADERS WHO CAN BUILD LEADERS

One of the most exciting findings is around leadership development. Organizations with compassionate leadership programs produce 76 percent more promotable leaders and have 43 percent better leadership succession rates (McCauley et al., 2010). When you lead with kindness, you're not just improving your own performance—you're modeling a way of leading that creates more great leaders.

These leadership programs ultimately lead to what researchers call "positive organizational energy"—a self-reinforcing cycle where good leadership creates more good leadership, high performance creates more high performance, and people flourishing creates more people flourishing.

THE TRUTH ABOUT COMPETITIVE KINDNESS

Look, I get it. When I first encountered this research, part of me was skeptical. It seemed too good to be true that you could be genuinely kind and caring while also driving exceptional results. The evidence is overwhelming, and more importantly, it makes intuitive sense when you really think about it.

When people feel valued, supported, and psychologically safe, they bring their best selves to work. When leaders model emotional regulation and genuine care, they create an environment where creativity flourishes, problems are solved faster, and everyone performs at a higher level. When organizations prioritize both human flourishing and business results, they create sustainable competitive advantages that their competitors can't replicate.

Neuroscience shows us that Competitive Kindness literally rewires our brains for better performance. Psychological research demonstrates that compassionate leaders make better decisions and recover from setbacks more quickly. Organizational studies prove that kind cultures drive better business results across every metric that matters.

It isn't about choosing between being kind or being successful—it's about understanding that at the highest levels of performance, they're the same thing. The research is clear. In our complex, interconnected business world, Competitive Kindness isn't just one leadership approach among many. It might just be the most scientifically validated path to sustainable excellence.

CHAPTER 6

COMPETITIVE KINDNESS VS. COMPETITIVE CRUELTY

We are in a championship battle between kindness and cruelty. Your choice for Competitive Kindness will not just shape quarterly results, but solidify your entire legacy.

"If we don't stand for something, we'll fall for anything."
Irene Dunne

Imagine that you're watching two CEOs present their quarterly results. Both hit their numbers. Both grew revenue. But here's what you don't see in those polished presentations—one built their success on the backs of exhausted, fearful employees, while the other cultivated a thriving culture where people want to show up on Monday morning. Adios Sunday Scaries!

As leaders, we face this fundamental choice every single day: will we lead through kindness or cruelty? And here's what I've discovered after years of research and real-world experience—while both approaches can drive short-term results, only one creates lasting success for our people, our organizations, and ourselves.

Let me show you why choosing Competitive Kindness isn't just the right thing to do, it's the most intelligent business decision you'll ever make.

TWO PATHS, TWO FATES

The difference between Competitive Kindness and Competitive Cruelty isn't just philosophical feel-good rhetoric—it's practical, measurable, and frankly striking when you see them side by side. Let's examine what these approaches look like in the real world:

DIMENSION	COMPETITIVE KINDNESS	COMPETITIVE CRUELTY
LEADERSHIP STYLE	Servant leadership, collaborative, empowering	Authoritarian, fear-based, micromanaging
MOTIVATIONAL CLIMATE	Purpose-driven, psychologically safe	Fear-driven, compliance-oriented
COMMUNICATION STYLE	Transparent, inclusive, constructive feedback	Polarizing, ambiguous, critical and public shaming
EMOTIONAL OUTCOMES	Trust, belonging, resilience	Anxiety, burnout, disengagement
PERFORMANCE IMPACT	Sustained high performance, innovation	Short-term compliance, long-term decline
TURNOVER AND RETENTION	Low turnover, strong loyalty	High turnover, toxic culture
REPUTATION	Employer of choice, strong brand loyalty	PR risks, brand attrition

When you see it laid out like this, the choice becomes obvious.

THE SURPRISING SCIENCE OF PSYCHOLOGICAL SAFETY

Here's something that might challenge your assumptions about high performance. Amy Edmondson's groundbreaking research shows us that psychological safety, not fear, is the secret ingredient for team effectiveness. When people feel safe to speak up, share ideas, and yes, even admit mistakes, something remarkable happens. Teams become learning machines, constantly improving and innovating.

But when fear rules the day? People go silent. They conform. They hide problems until they explode into disasters. The research is crystal clear on this.

CULTURE TYPE	EMPLOYEE BEHAVIOR	TEAM OUTCOME
PSYCHOLOGICAL SAFETY	Open feedback, innovation, risk-taking	High learning and performance
FEAR-BASED	Silence, conformity, fear of retaliation	Errors hidden, poor decision quality

Think about your own career for a moment. When did you do your most creative, innovative work? Was it when you felt supported and valued, or when you were walking on eggshells, afraid to make a mistake?

THE HIDDEN HUMAN COST OF OUR LEADERSHIP CHOICES

Let's talk about something that honestly keeps me up at night as a leader: the real human impact of our leadership choices. The research here isn't just eye-opening—it's a wake-up call.

Studies show that hostile leadership doesn't just hurt feelings, it literally makes people sick. We're talking about increased stress-related illnesses, more sick days, and people showing up physically but checking out mentally. As leaders, we're not just managing performance metrics; we're directly impacting human lives.

Here's the incredible flip side: compassionate leadership improves people's health. Lower cortisol levels, better immune function, and higher overall well-being. We have the power to heal or harm through our leadership approach, literally.

LEADERSHIP APPROACH	MENTAL HEALTH	PHYSICAL HEALTH	WELL-BEING
COMPETITIVE KINDNESS	Low anxiety, higher optimism	Improved immune function	High engagement, job satisfaction
COMPETITIVE CRUELTY	High anxiety, depression risk	Elevated cortisol, heart issues	Burnout, emotional exhaustion

As leaders, we hold people's well-being in our hands. That's not a responsibility any of us should take lightly.

THE LONG GAME: WHERE YOUR LEADERSHIP ACTUALLY TAKES YOU

With these facts in mind, the impact on the business world is fascinating. Studies have found that organizations built on the principles of Competitive Kindness create what's called "positive organizational energy." These places become magnets for top talent, innovation, and sustainable success.

This is where short-term thinking gets dangerous. Fear-based leadership might give you a quick performance bump as people scramble to avoid consequences, but it's like taking out a high-interest loan against your organization's future. The data shows that fear-based cultures eventually collapse under the weight of ethical lapses, plummeting morale, and mounting legal risks.

TIMELINE	COMPETITIVE KINDNESS PERFORMANCE	COMPETITIVE CRUELTY PERFORMANCE
YEAR 1	Moderate	High (Fear-based compliance)
YEAR 2	High	Medium
YEAR 3	High	Low
YEAR 4+	Sustained High	Declining

Look at that trajectory. Year one might feel like the cruel approach is winning, but by year three, kindness has not only caught up—it's pulling away. And it stays there.

WHY COMPETITIVE KINDNESS WINS EVERY SINGLE TIME

Let me be absolutely clear— Competitive Kindness is strong. Often described around the water cooler as "quiet strength." Competitive Kindness maintains the highest standards while treating people with dignity and respect.

When we lead with service, speak with purpose, and build with compassion, we unlock something extraordinary in people. We tap into their intrinsic motivation, their creativity, and their genuine desire to contribute to something meaningful. That's not just good leadership—that's exceptional business strategy.

The evidence isn't just compelling; it's overwhelming. Every metric that matters—performance, retention, innovation, reputation, financial results—favors the kind approach over the cruel one.

YOUR CHOICE, YOUR LEGACY

As you think about your own leadership journey, I want to leave you with this thought. The choice between Competitive Kindness and Competitive Cruelty isn't just about this quarter's results or this year's performance review. It's about the legacy you leave, the lives you touch, and the organization you build.

The research is clear, the business case is solid, and the impact on people is undeniable. When we choose kindness, we don't just create better workplaces—we build people around us to reach their human potential, one interaction at a time.

That's a competition worth winning.

THE CORE OF COMPETITIVE KINDNESS

> Competitive Kindness isn't some feel-good concept—
> it's a strategic advantage that lets you compete with relentless
> intensity while treating people with respect, creating cultures
> where people can win without sacrificing their soul.
>
> *"The love you liberate in your work is the love you keep."*
> Elbert Hubbard

At the heart of *Competitive Kindness* lies a simple but powerful truth—the kind of leader you are on the outside flows directly from who you are on the inside. Actual influence—the lasting, transformational type of influence—requires both inward conviction and outward compassion.

Ancient wisdom teaches us that this authentic leadership must begin with an internal transformation. As one timeless principle states, we must "cleanse first that which is within the cup and platter, that the outside of them may be clean also." External displays of leadership without genuine internal commitment ring hollow and ultimately fail. History's most extraordinary leaders understood that sustainable influence flows from character developed in private moments, not performance crafted for public consumption. Inward transformation is not optional—it is foundational.

The following chapters explore the principles that form the core of Competitive Kindness, divided into two vital expressions—the foundation and the pillars.

The Foundation Of Competitive Kindness (Inward Commitment)

These first three traits are deeply personal. They form the foundation of your character when no one is watching, when the cameras are off, and when the only person holding you accountable is you. They reflect a commitment to lead from the inside out—because you cannot give what you do not possess.

1. UNSHAKABLE INTEGRITY—DO WHAT IS RIGHT, EVEN WHEN IT'S HARD.

   Integrity is what you do when no one else will ever know—the late-night decision that may cost you money but saves your reputation. Leaders with unshakable integrity don't bend their values to fit circumstances; they shape circumstances to align with their values.

2. GENUINE AUTHENTICITY—LEAD FROM A PLACE OF SELF-AWARENESS.

   Authentic leaders know their strengths and own their weaknesses without pretending to have all the answers. When leaders show up as genuine human beings rather than polished personas, they create psychological safety that allows others to do the same.

3. THE HUMBLE CHAMPION—BE COACHABLE; PUT THE EGO IN CHECK TO HAVE A GROWTH MINDSET.

   Humble leadership is the internal strength to compete fiercely for your team's success while remaining genuinely open to learning and growth. Humility transforms traditional dynamics by competing alongside your people rather than against them for credit.

The Pillars of Competitive Kindness (Outward Manifestation)

The final five principles bring Competitive Kindness to life through visible leadership action. These traits show the world how strength and compassion not only can coexist—they must coexist if you want to build something that lasts. This is where your internal work translates into external impact.

1. VISION-DRIVEN ENCOURAGER – INSPIRE HOPE AND RALLY OTHERS AROUND A HIGHER PURPOSE.

   Great leaders don't just see what is, they see what they could be. They possess an unshakeable belief that the best is yet to come. Vision-driven encouragers paint pictures of a possibility so compelling that others want to pick up a brush and help create the masterpiece.

2. EMPOWER INDIVIDUAL WORTH – SEE THE POTENTIAL IN PEOPLE, NOT JUST THEIR PERFORMANCE.

   Every person has untapped potential waiting to be discovered and developed, and leaders who empower individual worth look beyond current capabilities to future possibilities. They understand that people don't care how much you know until they know how much you care about them as individuals.

3. ELEVATE OTHERS THROUGH SERVICE – USE POWER TO UPLIFT, NOT CONTROL.

   Servant leaders flip the traditional power pyramid upside down, serving others first instead of demanding service from them. They measure their success not by how many people serve them, but by how many people they've equipped to lead others.

4. SPEAK WITH PURPOSE – USE WORDS AS INSTRUMENTS OF CLARITY, NOT WEAPONS OF CRITICISM.

   Your words have power to build up or tear down, and leaders who speak with purpose choose them carefully to connect hearts and minds. They provide feedback that helps people grow rather than criticism that makes them shrink.

5. PURSUE EXCELLENCE WITH COMPASSION – SET HIGH STANDARDS WHILE SHOWING GRACE.

Excellence and compassion are complementary strengths that create leaders who demand the best from their teams while understanding that people are human beings, not machines. They set standards that stretch people without breaking them, holding people accountable while offering second chances.

In the chapters that follow, we'll dive deep into each of these eight traits. You'll discover not just what they mean, but how to develop them, when to apply them, and why they work. Each chapter includes real-world examples, practical tools, and research that validates the approach.

These eight traits are not soft. They are not passive. They are the hard-won disciplines of courageous, principled leaders who choose to compete with both fire and kindness. They are the foundation of cultures that win the right way and never lose their soul.

Let's explore the core of Competitive Kindness!

CHAPTER 8

UNSHAKABLE INTEGRITY

> Integrity isn't about choosing between success and ethics—in the long run, they're the same thing. Your consistency becomes your currency and your integrity becomes your legacy.
>
> *"The supreme quality for leadership is unquestionably integrity. Without it, no real success is possible, no matter whether it is on a section gang, a football field, in an army, or in an office."*
> Dwight D. Eisenhower

In today's hyperconnected business environment where every decision can be scrutinized by millions within hours, integrity isn't just a moral imperative, it's the foundation for Competitive Kindness. Yet integrity remains one of the most misunderstood concepts in leadership development. It's not about perfection, grand gestures, or public declarations. It's about the quiet consistency that builds unshakeable trust.

THE BOBBY JONES MOMENT: WHEN CHARACTER DEFINES LEGACY

Let me share a story that has influenced my leadership mindset on integrity for decades. In 1925, golfing legend Bobby Jones was competing for the U.S. Open championship. During a crucial moment, his club barely touched his ball in an almost imperceptible movement that no official noticed, no competitor saw, and no camera recorded.

Jones faced a choice that would define not only his tournament but also his entire legacy. He could remain silent and continue playing or call a penalty on himself and sacrifice his chance at victory. Without hesitation, Jones penalized himself for one stroke. That one stroke cost him the U.S. Open championship that year. When interviewed by the media and praised for his honesty, his response was characteristically humble: "You might as well praise a man for not robbing a bank."

This moment illustrates what Harvard Business School professor Frances Hesselbein calls "authentic leadership"—the alignment between our deepest values and our most visible actions. Jones understood that integrity isn't about the audience, rather it's about the alignment between who we are when no one is watching and who we claim to be when the eyes of the public are upon us.

REDEFINING INTEGRITY FOR MODERN LEADERS

The word "integrity" derives from the Latin *integritas*, meaning wholeness or completeness. In business terms, think of integrity as the absence of gaps between your private convictions and your public decisions. It's what Warren Buffett describes as "the quality of being whole and undivided"—a leader whose Monday morning staff meeting reflects the same values as their Sunday evening family dinner.

Oftentimes, people try to separate their work lives from their personal lives. As much as that compartmentalization sounds logical, it weakens people at the core and places all that they seek to do and become at risk because of incongruency.

But here's what makes integrity truly powerful in today's business climate: it eliminates the cognitive load of inconsistency. When your team knows you'll make decisions based on consistent principles rather than shifting circumstances, they can redirect their mental energy from second-guessing your motives to focusing on performance and innovation.

Research from the Center for Creative Leadership confirms that integrity-based leadership isn't just morally superior—it's strategically advantageous. Their longitudinal study of Fortune 500 executives found that leaders who consistently demonstrated integrity achieved 2.3 times higher employee engagement scores and 40 percent lower voluntary turnover rates.

THE SCIENCE OF TRUST COMPOUNDING

Jim Kouzes and Barry Posner's seminal research in *The Leadership Challenge* revealed a striking finding. When they asked people what qualities are most wanted in a leader, credibility rooted in integrity ranked above intelligence, vision, and even competence. This isn't sentiment; it's strategic reality.

Consider the neuroscience behind trust. When we interact with someone we perceive as trustworthy, our brains release oxytocin, often called the "trust or love hormone." This neurochemical response reduces stress, increases collaboration, and enhances creative problem-solving. Conversely, when we question someone's integrity, our amygdala triggers a stress response that impairs cognitive function and team performance.

Stephen Covey captured this perfectly stating, "Trust is the glue of life. It's the most essential ingredient in effective communication. It's the foundational principle that holds all relationships." From a purely business perspective, integrity isn't just the right thing to do—it's the profitable thing to do. Integrity is more than just good business.

THE MORAL OR SPIRITUAL JOURNEY OF INTEGRITY

The philosopher Pierre Teilhard de Chardin said, "We are not human beings having a spiritual experience; we are spiritual beings having a human experience." Your journey in the fields of competition is a moral or spiritual journey to its core. With this perspective, we must transform how we think about integrity. We're not simply winning championships or achieving career goals—we're becoming someone through every choice we make. Integrity is the foundation upon which trust is built, not through grand gestures, but through the steady accumulation of aligned actions.

When our decisions reflect our stated values, no matter if anyone is watching, we create a pattern of reliability where others can depend on us. Each choice, from how we handle a difficult conversation to whether we take credit we haven't earned, becomes a small investment in the person and leader we're becoming. This is where character is fostered. Trust is built in the countless unseen moments where we choose consistency over convenience. And that consistent integrity doesn't just build trust with others—it builds trust with ourselves, creating the confidence to lead with both strength and kindness. Integrity empowers you to look at yourself in the mirror with confidence knowing that you are becoming the best version of yourself.

HOW TO BUILD YOUR INTEGRITY FOUNDATION

Now, let's be clear that integrity isn't a personality trait you're born with, but rather a character competency you develop through deliberate practice. Here's how the most effective leaders that I've worked with and observed have built and maintained their integrity.

1. Define Your Non-Negotiables

Before you face your next ethical test, establish what you stand for. Research from the University of Pennsylvania's Wharton School shows that leaders with clearly defined values make decisions 60 percent faster and experience significantly less decision fatigue.

Take time this week to identify three to five core principles that will guide your decisions regardless of external pressure. Write them down. Share them with your loved ones. Share them with your leadership team.

Make them part of your team's DNA, both at home and in your fields of competition.

2. Practice Micro-Integrity

Integrity is built in the seemingly insignificant moments. It's following through on the small commitments—returning calls when promised, giving credit to others where due, or admitting when you don't know something. These daily choices create what psychologists call "behavioral consistency," which builds predictability and trust over time.

As Maya Angelou wisely observed, "I've learned that people will forget what you said, people will forget what you did, but people will never forget how you made them feel." Micro-integrity moments shape how people feel about your leadership long before the major decisions arise. It's how Bobby Jones turned one mishap at a tournament into a legendary golf career with integrity.

3. Cultivate Courageous Conversations

Surround yourself with people who will challenge your thinking and hold you accountable. The most successful leaders actively seek feedback and create psychological safety for dissenting opinions. This isn't about being liked—it's about being effective.

Research from Google's *Project Aristotle* found that psychological safety—the belief that you can speak up without risk of punishment or humiliation—is the top factor in team effectiveness. Leaders with unshakeable integrity don't just tolerate difficult conversations; they invite them.

HOW INTEGRITY IS YOUR COMPETITIVE ADVANTAGE

Your integrity will be tested most when the stakes are the highest and the ethical choice is most costly. These moments rarely come with clear labels or obvious answers. They arrive disguised as business decisions, personnel choices, or strategic pivots.

You might face pressure to inflate quarterly numbers to meet investor expectations. You could encounter opportunities to gain competitive intelligence through questionable means. You may need to choose between protecting a loyal employee and protecting your team's performance.

In these moments, remember that integrity isn't about finding the perfect solution—it's about making decisions you can defend not just to your board, but to your children. As Albert Einstein noted, "Try not to become a person of success, but rather try to become a person of value."

INTEGRITY LEADS TO AUTHENTIC LEADERSHIP

When you lead with unshakeable integrity, you don't just change your organization—you influence your entire ecosystem. Suppliers begin to trust your commitments. Customers become brand advocates. Competitors respect your approach even when they disagree with your decisions.

It becomes like an "integrity dividend"—where the compound return on consistent ethical leadership becomes your authentic identity. A study by the Harvard Business Review found that companies with strong ethical cultures experience 2.5 times higher stock performance and significantly lower regulatory violations.

More importantly, you create what researchers call "moral elevation" in others—the tendency for ethical behavior to inspire similar behavior in those who witness it. Your integrity literally becomes contagious, elevating the ethical standards of everyone in your sphere of influence.

PRACTICAL IMPLICATIONS

Before we move forward, here are three practical tools to help you build and maintain unshakeable integrity in your quest for Competitive Kindness:

1. The Integrity Audit

Periodically, assess your decisions against your stated values. Ask yourself: Where have I been tempted to compromise? What behaviors are misaligned with my stated principles? It isn't about perfection—it's about awareness and course correction as missteps arise.

2. The Transparency Test

Before making major decisions, ask yourself these three questions. Is this consistent with my core values? Can I explain this decision publicly? Does this honor the dignity and worth of everyone affected? If you can't answer "yes" to all three, reconsider your approach.

3. The Legacy Filter

Consider how you want to be remembered as a leader. Then ask yourself: do my current actions align with how I want to be remembered? It isn't about ego—it's about ensuring your daily choices reflect your deepest aspirations for leadership impact.

THE LEADER WORTH FOLLOWING

Here's the ultimate litmus test regarding your integrity as a leader: "Would I want to work for me?" Not the leader you aspire to be someday, but the one you are *right now* in the difficult moments when your values are tested.

Unshakeable integrity isn't about moral superiority—it's a matter of strategic effectiveness. It's about understanding that in a world where trust is scarce and skepticism is abundant, chaos and pressure abound, your consistency becomes your currency.

The leaders who master this don't just build better businesses—they develop better people. They prove that Competitive Kindness isn't about choosing between success and integrity; it's about understanding that in the long run, they're the same thing.

Your integrity is your legacy. Make it unshakeable.

CHAPTER 9

GENUINE AUTHENTICITY

Be yourself. Genuinely care about others and commit to getting better every day. Lead with sincerity, consistency, and vulnerability. This is foundational to competitive kindness.

"To be yourself in a world that is constantly trying to make you something else is the greatest accomplishment."
Ralph Waldo Emerson

WHY BEING REAL IS THE FOUNDATION OF COMPETITIVE KINDNESS

People don't follow with their hearts because of your title—they follow you. And the "you" they're looking for isn't the polished, perfect Instagram version of you that you think they want to see. They're looking for the real deal.

In my years working with executives across industries, I have observed countless leaders exhausting themselves trying to be someone they're not. They study other successful leaders, adopt their mannerisms, and wonder why their teams aren't responding. Meanwhile, the leaders who make the most profound impact are those brave enough to show up as themselves—complete with their quirks, their learning edges, and their genuine care for others. Genuine authenticity is fundamentally about creating that feeling of trust, safety, and authentic connection.

THE ZOOM ROOM THAT CHANGED THE GAME

It started with a question that had echoed for decades in locker rooms and coaching offices across the country: "Where are all the Black head coaches?"

Coach Alonzo Carter didn't ask the question with cynicism. He asked it with conviction and authenticity. A former hip-hop dancer who once performed on stage with MC Hammer, Carter had evolved into a dynamic running backs coach at San José State. He had walked an uncommon path to college football and never pretended to be anything other than who he was: a bold, empathetic leader with a relentless work ethic and a deep love for people. That genuine authenticity became his superpower.

Carter had experienced the game from almost every angle—youth coach, high school head coach, junior college program-builder, Division I position coach. He had seen how Black coaches were often left out of the rooms where decisions were made—not for lack of talent, but because there was no pipeline, no visibility, no community.

As COVID-19 halted practices and cleared schedules, Carter stepped up, not for credit, but for connection. He opened his laptop and started a Zoom series—often referred to as "The West Coast Zoom Call"—a virtual meet-up to connect Black football coaches across all levels: high school, JUCO, FCS, FBS, and the NFL. There were no corporate sponsors. No marketing budget. Just a genuine invitation: "Pull up a seat. Let's build together."

At first, a handful of California-based coaches joined in. But within weeks, the word spread. Dozens, then hundreds of Black coaches started logging in weekly. His pool of football coaches expanded to all ethnic minorities.

Some had never had a mentor. Others had never shared their story. But this Zoom room became something rare in the competitive world of football: a space to be seen, to be real, and to be yourself.

To genuinely make an impact, Carter hosted guests each week—current head coaches, athletic directors, NFL personnel, search firm leaders—who shared knowledge, gave feedback, and answered questions honestly. No filters. No corporate gloss. Just truth, trust, and transparency.

"There's enough success to go around," Carter said. "We're not here to compete with each other—we're here to complete each other." What set Carter's Zoom movement apart was not just the information being shared, but how it was shared. It was real talk. It was vulnerable and encouraging, with zero ego.

Carter modeled what genuine authenticity—one of the core pillars of Competitive Kindness—looks like in leadership:

- He didn't pretend to have all the answers.
- He didn't create hierarchy or competition.
- He brought his whole self to the table and invited others to do
  the same

In doing so, he created a community where coaches didn't have to perform—they could belong. That belonging led to momentum: new job opportunities, mentor relationships, and broader visibility for dozens of coaches who had long operated in the margins. Coaches like Maurice Linguist (then at Buffalo) and Charles Huff (then at Marshall) shared their journeys. Young assistants learned how to navigate interviews. Veterans passed on wisdom. Everyone grew.

Carter's Zoom initiative wasn't about building his brand. In fact, it took him several more challenging years of hard work as an assistant coach before he became a Division I coach. The Zoom was all about creating a bridge—from isolation to opportunity, from silence to visibility, from exclusion to belonging. He reminds us of something increasingly rare in leadership: when you show up as your authentic self, you permit others to do the same. Authentic leadership is never about image—it's about building up the people around you with Competitive Kindness to help them become reach their potential. No jealousy. Not to be noticed. Simply because it's the right thing to do and knowing that real change begins with being real.

THE SCIENCE BEHIND AUTHENTICITY

Let's talk numbers for a moment, because authenticity isn't just a feel-good concept, it's backed by serious research. In a comprehensive study by Walumbwa and colleagues, researchers found that leaders demonstrating genuine authenticity drive remarkable results in the workplace:

- 32 percent increase in job satisfaction
- 28 percent boost in organizational commitment
- 25 percent improvement in psychological well-being
- 18 percent enhancement in performance metrics

Neuroscience also confirms the positive impact of being genuine. Neuroscientist Paul Zak found that when people perceive authenticity, their brains release oxytocin (the "trust hormone"). This neurochemical response literally makes people more cooperative, more creative, and more willing to go the extra mile.

On the flip side, when people sense that someone is being fake, their amygdala—the brain's alarm system—kicks into high gear, creating resistance and disengagement. Think about it: your team's brains are constantly scanning for whether you're the real deal or just putting on a show. If you are being fake, their brains will kick into fight or flight mode. Then, good luck trying to build trust when that's happening.

Additionally, the people you lead want to know if you genuinely have their best interest at heart. As Harvard Business School's Bill George said in *Authentic Leadership*, "Authentic leaders genuinely desire to serve others through their leadership. They are more concerned with empowering the people they lead to make a difference than they are with their own power, money, or prestige." Genuinely authentic leaders are not only real—they must also genuinely serve and care about the wellbeing of the people they lead.

When you lead authentically, you permit others to bring their whole selves to work. You create environments where people don't just perform, they flourish. Research from Gallup's *State of the Global Workplace* shows that teams with authentic leaders are five times more likely to be engaged, three times more likely to be high performing, and have 40 percent lower turnover.

But beyond the metrics, there's something deeper at work. When you show up as your genuine self—values-driven, growth-oriented, and genuinely caring—you create what I call "permission to be real," where people around you start to relax into who they really are, bringing their best ideas, their unique perspectives, and their whole hearts to the work.

THE FOUR KEYS TO GENUINE AUTHENTICITY

Based on Avolio and Gardner's foundational research, authenticity rests on four keys:

1. Self-Awareness

Knowing your strengths, blind spots, and impact on others. It isn't about being perfect—it's about being honest about who you are and who you're becoming.

2. Relational Transparency

Being open and genuine in your interactions.

3. Balanced Processing

Seeking diverse perspectives before making decisions. It means checking your biases and creating space for voices that might challenge your thinking.

4. Moral Perspective

Acting from a clear set of values and ethical principles, especially when it's inconvenient or costly.

BUILDING YOUR AUTHENTICITY MUSCLE

I get it. It is easy to say "Be yourself" while you might be asking yourself who you really are to your core. That's normal. Don't beat yourself up about that. Instead, let's work through this together to build up your authentic self, so you can be genuine.

1. Get Clear on Your Core Values

Your integrity and authenticity are inextricably connected. So, start with this question: what do you stand for when no one's watching? Not just your aspirational values, but your non-negotiables—the principles you won't compromise on even under pressure.

2. Master the Art of Strategic Vulnerability

Here's where many leaders get it wrong. They think authenticity means oversharing or being raw all the time. That's not it.

Strategic vulnerability, as researcher Brené Brown explains, is about sharing your struggles and growth in service of connection and learning—not for sympathy or attention. Brown said, "Vulnerability is not winning or losing; it's having the courage to show up and be seen when we have no control over the outcome."

There are four elements of sharing vulnerability through storytelling to prevent oversharing and maximize connection with others through genuine authenticity:

1. Challenge: What obstacle did you face?
2. Choice: What decision did you make and why?
3. Consequence: What happened as a result?
4. Change: What did you learn and how did you grow?

These stories, shared at the right moments, don't diminish your credibility—they enhance it.

3. Drop the Performance and Be Present

The most exhausting thing about leadership isn't the long hours or tough decisions, it's trying to be someone you're not. Adam Grant, in *Give and Take*, found that leaders who consistently show up as themselves (the same values, same personality, same care for others across all contexts) build what he calls "authentic influence."

It takes intentionality to approach being yourself. When it becomes challenging to do so, ask yourself these questions to ensure that you are present in the moment:

- Am I the same person in the boardroom and the break room?
- What masks am I wearing, and why?
- Where am I trying to impress, instead of connect with people?
- How can I show up more genuinely tomorrow?

4. Choose Growth Over Image

When your goal is to "look like a leader," you become performative. When your goal is to "grow as a leader," you become powerful. Carol Dweck's research on growth mindset shows that leaders who openly acknowledge their learning edges and actively seek feedback create more innovative, resilient teams. But keep in mind that the type of feedback you might need from others and yourself can sometimes sting. The key is to continue seeking ways to get better every day. With a growth mindset, you must be willing to sacrifice the fear of looking stupid to improve every day.

If you're wondering whether you have a growth mindset or you are choosing image over personal growth, ask yourself:

- What am I learning this week?
- Who am I learning from?
- What feedback am I actively seeking?
- How am I sharing my learning journey with others?

WHEN AUTHENTICITY MATTERS MOST

There are times in your Competitive Kindness journey where some will need your genuine authenticity more than others. In these moments, people look to someone real they can lean on to overcome adversity.

1. During Crisis and Uncertainty

When people are anxious about the future, they need leaders who are honest about what they know and what they don't. As Jim Collins writes in *Good to Great*, high-level leaders who are authentic "look out the window to apportion credit to factors outside themselves when things go well, and look in the mirror to apportion responsibility, never blaming bad luck when things go poorly". If things go wrong, own it. If things go right, share the success.

2. In Moments of Conflict

Authentic leaders acknowledge their role in problems and focus on solutions rather than blame. It creates psychological safety for others to own their contributions, too. When you blame others, complain about conflict, or become defensive, you become a weakened, inauthentic leader.

3. While Building New Relationships

First impressions matter, but authentic leaders focus on making genuine connections rather than trying to impress. It creates a foundation for deeper, more productive partnerships. Seek connection to be authentic.

CREATING SPACE FOR OTHERS' AUTHENTICITY

Competitive Kindness isn't just about being authentic yourself—it's about celebrating authenticity in others. Bob Beaudine said that the people you lead will follow this mantra: "Go to where you are celebrated, not just merely tolerated." The authentic leader who is competitively kind will celebrate others' authenticity by:

- Making room for different voices, stories, and leadership styles
- Valuing contributions over conformity
- Creating psychological safety where people can express themselves without fear
- Celebrating people not just for what they do, but who they're becoming

By creating space for others' true selves, you will make a psychologically safe environment for high-performing teams—not just a friendly space. As Google's *Project Aristotle* research revealed, psychological safety created through authentic leadership is the most critical factor in high-performing teams. So how does this work in practice?

In Daily Interactions

- An executive asking their direct report how they're really doing—and listening with full attention
- A coach admitting they missed the mark—and using it as a teaching moment
- A manager choosing encouragement over ego—because they care more about growth than credit

In Team Meetings

- Starting with genuine check-ins, not just agenda items
- Acknowledging when you don't have all the answers
- Asking for input and actually incorporating it into decisions

During Performance Conversations

- Sharing your own development goals alongside your team members'
- Being honest about organizational challenges while maintaining hope
- Focusing on growth trajectories, not just current performance

THE HEART OF IT ALL

Genuine authenticity isn't a leadership technique—it's a personal transformation. It's the daily choice to be real (rooted in your values) and to be relatable to those you serve.

In a world full of leaders trying to be someone else, the most radical—and most potent—thing you can do is be genuinely, courageously yourself.

That's why genuine authenticity is foundational to Competitive Kindness. Authenticity is where trust is built and where transformation happens—one authentic interaction at a time.

THE HUMBLE CHAMPION

> Linked with integrity and authenticity, humility might be your greatest competitive advantage. Humility drives inner strength that beats outer noise. Watch what happens when leaders choose quiet confidence over loud ego
>
> *"True nobility is not about being superior to another man. True nobility is being superior to your former self."*
> Ernest Hemingway

A STORY OF THE HUMBLE CHAMPION

The stadium in Stockholm grew tense as Alma Richards, an unassuming farm boy from the small town of Parowan, Utah, prepared for his final attempt at the high jump bar. The 1912 Olympics had come down to this—a 22-year-old who seemed an unlikely competitor among the world's most accomplished athletes. In fact, a few of his fellow athletes while aboard a ship sailing to the games, had amused themselves by prodding the "raw youngster" and mocking him as a "hick" because of his country upbringing on a farm. What happened next defied every prediction and rewrote the story of Olympic greatness.

After the failure of the world record holder, George Horine, to clear 6 ft. 3¼ in., Richards and Hans Liesche of Germany battled it out for the high jump gold medal. The pressure was immense. It wasn't just about personal glory—Richards carried the hopes of his small Utah town, his college, and everyone who had believed in the quiet farm boy when others had written him off.

But Richards' approach to this defining moment revealed the humble character that had brought him this far. While other competitors paced anxiously, psyching themselves up with aggressive displays of confidence, Richards stood quietly, his eyes closed in calm prayer, preparing. Those that should have been his teammates offered much more criticism than camaraderie for a boy they saw as "a little too country" and "a little too churchy."

Instead of letting their mockery fuel bitterness or arrogance, Richards had spent the entire Olympics quietly observing, learning from every competitor. He studied their techniques, asked them questions to learn, and even offered encouragement to rivals who had initially dismissed him. Doing a lot with a little and doing it with humility is what made Richards a stand-out.

Richards cleared 6 ft. 4 in. (1.93m) on his final attempt and, with Liesche failing three times, the gold medal went to the humble farm boy. His Olympic record would stand for years, but what happened immediately after his victory revealed the true measure of the man.

Instead of celebrating wildly or boasting about his triumph over the doubters, Richards' first act was to walk over to the German competitor who had pushed him to greatness. He offered his hand and spoke words of respect for Liesche's performance. When reporters asked about his victory, Richards deflected credit to his coaches, his family, and even his competitors, who had "made him better by challenging him to rise higher." He was truly a humble champion.

But it didn't stop at the Olympics. After graduating from Cornell University with a law degree, he taught science at Venice High School in

Los Angeles for thirty-two years. Richards turned down opportunities for fame and fortune, choosing instead to invest his life in young people, using his Olympic story not to aggrandize himself but to inspire students to believe in their own potential.

Years later, former students would remember not the gold medal that occasionally sat on his desk, but the way their teacher had made each of them feel capable of clearing bars they never thought possible. True to form, Richards requested to be buried in the simple Parowan Cemetery where his Olympic journey had begun—the humble champion who understood that real victory wasn't about standing above others but about lifting others alongside you in life's journey.

THE PARADOX OF THE HUMBLE CHAMPION

While seemingly contradictory, the most competitive people I know are often the most humble. Not humble in a self-deprecating, "aw shucks" kind of way or even in a humble brag sort of way, but humble in the truest sense. They possess an accurate understanding of their strengths and limitations, and they're secure enough to let their work speak louder than their words.

This isn't weakness. It's wisdom. As faith-leader Gordon B. Hinckley said, "Humility is not about thinking less of yourself. It's about thinking of yourself less." And it's becoming one of the most powerful differentiators in leadership today. Researchers from the University of Washington confirmed this by finding that humble leaders create teams with 12 percent better performance outcomes and 40 percent higher employee retention rates. Why? Because humility creates psychological safety, and psychological safety unleashes potential.

EGO: THE HIDDEN PERFORMANCE KILLER

To understand why humility creates such a competitive advantage, we must first examine its opposite: ego-driven leadership. Dr. Ryan Holiday, in his seminal work "Ego Is the Enemy," presents compelling evidence that ego consistently undermines performance and sustainable success. But the damage runs deeper than individual failure—it creates what organizational psychologists call "defensive climates."

These defensive climates have been found to wreak havoc on organizations. Research by Dr. Jack Gibb found that ego-driven leaders create environments characterized by evaluation, control, and superiority—conditions that trigger defensive responses in team members. When people feel they must protect themselves from their leader's ego, cognitive resources that could be devoted to innovation, collaboration, and problem-solving are instead consumed by self-protection. Additionally, Dr. Kristin Neff's groundbreaking research on self-compassion provides the neurological evidence: ego-driven thinking activates the brain's threat detection system, flooding the neural pathways with cortisol and adrenaline. These stress hormones literally impair higher-order thinking, creativity, and emotional regulation. In contrast, humble self-awareness activates the brain's caregiving system, releasing oxytocin and promoting the cognitive flexibility essential for complex problem-solving. The implications are staggering—ego doesn't just make leaders less likable; it makes their entire organization less intelligent.

THE NEUROSCIENCE OF HUMBLE LEADERSHIP

If that wasn't enough evidence, let's ramp this up another notch with neuroscience. Recent research revealed that humility can actually change how our brains process information. When we operate from a place of ego, our brains are constantly scanning for threats to our self-image. It creates what researchers call "cognitive load"—mental energy that could be better used for problem-solving, creativity, and connection. Dr. David Rock's research through the NeuroLeadership Institute shows that humble leaders have lower cortisol levels and higher cognitive flexibility. They literally think better because they're not spending mental energy protecting their ego.

If you want to be more strategic, humility is key. Dr. Mary Kern's longitudinal studies at UC Berkeley found that leaders who scored higher on humility assessments demonstrated superior pattern recognition, more accurate risk assessment, and better long-term strategic thinking. The reason? Their brains weren't hijacked by the constant need to maintain self-image. Think about that for a moment. Humility isn't just morally admirable—it's cognitively advantageous.

THE INTERNAL ARCHITECTURE OF HUMILITY

As a core tenet of Competitive Kindness, genuine humility isn't a performance. It's an internal filter that shows up in how you process success, handle failure, and relate to others. Dr. Bradley Owens, whose research on humble leadership has shaped our understanding of this trait, identifies three core components:

1. Accurate Self-Assessment

Humble leaders know their strengths without inflating them and acknowledge their weaknesses without being paralyzed by them. They can say "I don't know" without feeling diminished. This accurate self-perception creates what psychologists call "cognitive calibration"—the ability to assess situations and make decisions based on reality rather than wishful thinking.

2. Appreciation of Others

They genuinely recognize and value their team members' contributions. This isn't strategic flattery—it's authentic recognition that everyone brings something valuable to the table. Dr. Adam Grant's research reveals that this appreciation creates "prosocial motivation," where team members become genuinely invested in collective success rather than solely individual advancement.

3. Teachability

Perhaps most importantly, they remain open to learning, feedback, and growth. As psychologist Carol Dweck notes in her research on growth mindset, "The hallmark of successful individuals and organizations is that they are constantly learning." This teachability creates what organizational theorists call "adaptive capacity"—the ability to evolve strategies and approaches in response to new information.

HUMILITY AS A FOUNDATION OF COMPETITIVE KINDNESS

Here's where humility becomes the secret weapon of Competitive Kindness. Humility transforms competition from a zero-sum game into a positive-sum opportunity. When leaders operate from humility, they're not competing to prove their superiority—they're competing to unlock their organization's full potential.

Dr. Monica Worline's research at Stanford reveals that humble leaders create "compassionate climates" where competitive energy is channeled toward collective achievement rather than individual dominance. These environments don't eliminate competition—they elevate it. Teams compete to contribute more value, to serve customers better, to solve more complex problems together.

The research is clear. Organizations led by humble leaders don't just outperform ego-driven competitors, they create sustainable competitive advantages that compound over time. Why? Because humility builds what Harvard's Frances Frei calls "trust multipliers"—conditions that enable rapid learning, authentic collaboration, and resilient innovation.

HUMILITY UNLOCKS QUIET CONFIDENCE

I've worked with leaders across industries—from Fortune 500 CEOs to championship coaches—and the pattern is consistent: the most sustainably successful ones lead with quiet confidence. They don't need to be the most intelligent person in the room because they are not afraid to hire people who are excellent or even more intelligent than they are. They don't need to take credit because they understand that shared success multiplies faster than hoarded recognition.

Consider the research from Jim Collins in *Good to Great*. His Level 5 leaders—those who took companies from good to great performance—were characterized by what he called "a paradoxical blend of personal humility and professional will." The top leaders in the study were ambitious, but their ambition was primarily for the organization, not themselves. Humility isn't about being passive or lacking confidence. As Maya Angelou beautifully put it: "Successful people have no fear of being vulnerable. They dare to be imperfect, to be uncertain, and to be open to learning." This courage is the quiet confidence to be humble.

HUMILITY ACTIVATES THE TRUST MULTIPLIER EFFECT

Here's what happens when humility becomes your leadership operating system: trust multiplies exponentially. And trust, as we know, is the foundation of all high-performing teams.

Dr. Amy Edmondson's research on psychological safety found that when leaders model vulnerability and admit their mistakes, team members are 67 percent more likely to speak up with ideas, concerns, and innovations. They're also 27 percent more likely to stay with the organization long-term. Why? Because humility signals safety. When team members see their leader acknowledge uncertainty or admit error, it permits them to be human too. And humans who feel safe to be human do their best work.

THE HUMILITY HABITS OF GREAT LEADERS

So how do you cultivate this internal strength? Here are the practices I've observed in leaders who embody Competitive Kindness through humility:

The Daily Question

Every morning, before checking email or diving into tasks, ask: "What can I learn today, and how can I serve others?" This simple practice shifts your brain from ego-protection mode to growth mode.

The Credit Redirect

When praised for team achievements, practice the "credit redirect." Instead of only saying "Thank you," try "I'm grateful to work with such a talented team. Let me tell you about the people who made this possible."

The Curiosity Conversation

Schedule regular one-on-ones where your only agenda is learning. Ask your team: "What am I missing?" "Where could we improve?" "What would you do differently if you were in my position?"

The Failure Debrief

When things go wrong, model the behavior you want to see. Try saying, "I made a mistake. Here's what I learned. Here's what I'll do differently next time." This creates a culture where failure becomes fuel for growth rather than a source of shame.

The Wisdom Circle

Create regular forums where team members can share insights, challenges, and lessons learned without judgment. Position yourself as a fellow learner rather than the source of all wisdom.

THE RIPPLE EFFECT OF HUMBLE LEADERSHIP

Something remarkable happens when you lead with humility—it becomes contagious. Dr. Adam Grant found that humble leaders create "prosocial cascades," where their humility encourages similar behavior in others, creating a positive feedback loop throughout the organization.

I've seen this in action. When I asked a CEO for advice, he told me he started every meeting by sharing something he'd learned from one team member that month. Within six months, his entire leadership team had adopted similar practices. Within a year, their employee engagement scores nearly doubled, and their customer satisfaction ratings reached all-time highs.

The internal work of humility—the quiet confidence, the accurate self-assessment, the genuine appreciation for others—creates external results that ego-driven leadership can't match.

Richards' Olympic story illustrates this perfectly. His humble response to mockery and criticism with quiet observation and genuine respect for competitors didn't weaken his performance, it unleashed a level of focus and determination that pure individual ambition never could have accessed. This is the paradox of Competitive Kindness. When we compete to elevate ourselves while maintaining respect for others, we discover capabilities we never knew we had.

THE LONG GAME ADVANTAGE

Here's the beautiful truth about humility: it's built for the long game. Ego-driven leadership might create short-term wins, but it's ultimately unsustainable. People leave. Trust erodes. Innovation stagnates. On the other hand, humble leadership compounds over time. As the Tao Te Ching teaches: "The sage does not attempt anything very big, and thus achieves greatness."

The most competitive thing you can do is build a culture where everyone feels valued, heard, and challenged to grow. That's not soft leadership—that's visionary leadership. And in an economy where sustainable competitive advantage increasingly comes from the ability to adapt, learn, and innovate collectively, humility isn't just a nice-to-have virtue—it's a business imperative.

Richards understood this intuitively in that defining moment at the 1912 Stockholm Olympics. He demonstrated what Competitive Kindness looks like when the stakes are highest. True champions don't just clear the highest bars; they inspire others to believe they can jump higher than they ever imagined.

Because any competitive leader can be prone to ego, we all need to keep ourselves in check. These reflection questions can be a source not only for keeping your ego in check but also for resetting you on your humility journey toward Competitive Kindness.

- **Inner Assessment:** Where does your ego show up most in your leadership? What would change if you approached that area with more humility?
- **Growth Mindset:** When was the last time you said "I don't know" or "I was wrong" to your team? How did it feel, and how did they respond?
- **Credit Distribution:** Think about a recent success. How did you share credit? What would you do differently next time?
- **Learning Posture:** What's one area where you could become more teachable? Who on your team could help you grow in that area?
- **Ego Check:** What triggers your defensive responses? How might those same situations become opportunities to model humility and create psychological safety?

Remember: Humility isn't about thinking less of yourself—it's about thinking of yourself less. And that shift in perspective is foundational to becoming the competitively kind leader who will change the world for the people you lead.

CHAPTER 11

VISION-DRIVEN ENCOURAGER

The vision-driven encourager transforms lives by helping people see their own potential, even when they may not see it in themselves.

"Great leaders don't just see what is—they see what could be, possessing an unshakable belief that the best is yet to come. Vision-driven encouragers paint pictures of possibility so compelling that others want to pick up a brush and help create the masterpiece."

VISION FROM THE COURT TO THE COURTROOM

The rowdy fans in the Chicago gymnasium fell silent. With fifteen seconds left and the national championship on the line and every eye was on Rulon "Bunny" Clark—the 1916 University of Utah basketball team's captain and forward. Clark had the ball and, seemingly, the shot; after all, he had earned the right to take it. But Clark saw something others missed. His teammate, Clyde Packer, was positioned perfectly under the basket, hands ready, eyes focused—a player who had been working all season to prove himself in crucial moments. Where others saw pressure, Clark saw his teammate's potential finally ready to shine for the team. He passed the ball. His teammate scored. Utah won. When asked by the newspapers about their win, Clark revealed true vision: "We had ten wonderful fellows on the team, but no stars. We won because we were all equal and all played our hearts out for Coach, the school, and the state." He saw the champion within his teammates long before anyone else did.

Forty-three years later, Judge "Bunny" Clark now sat behind a Utah juvenile court bench; his philosophy of seeing the hidden potential in people remained unchanged. A sixteen-year-old boy stood before him. He had been caught burglarizing homes after his father abandoned the family. The law prescribed punishment, but Judge Clark saw something else entirely—a young man whose desperate circumstances had obscured his true character. While he did not condone the illegal behavior, Judge Clark showed mercy and demonstrated that, with hard work, this young man could change the trajectory of his life and become a productive citizen. A few years later, this young man sent this in a letter to Judge Clark:

"There is a strain of good in each of us and a desire to live on the highest level we can. Sometimes the good is hidden due to a wrong environment, emotional stress, childhood bitterness, or neglect. Judge Clark, you have discovered the better traits of youth and saved the youths themselves so they could live free and be able to achieve happiness as you did for me."

What made Judge Clark a vision-driven encourager wasn't his position of authority—it was his extraordinary ability to see people's potential before they could see it themselves. On the basketball court, he created moments for teammates to discover their own greatness. In the courtroom, he created pathways for people to transform their lives. He understood that true competitive advantage doesn't come from diminishing others, but from helping them become the best versions of themselves. That pass in 1916 didn't just win one national championship game—it gave a teammate a defining moment that shaped his confidence for life. That courtroom decision didn't just save one young man—it revealed his true character to himself and launched a transformation that spanned generations.

This is the power of vision-driven encouragement in Competitive Kindness. Vision-driven encouragers transform lives by helping people see their own potential. Judge Clark showed us that the most powerful question a leader can ask isn't "How can I win?" but "What do I see in this person that they can't yet see in themselves?" His legacy lived not in personal achievements, but in the countless moments when someone discovered their own capability because he first believed in it. When someone chooses to see potential instead of problems, to speak to someone's future rather than their past, to encourage growth rather than simply demanding performance—that's when Competitive Kindness transforms from a strategy into a force that awakens the best in people across generations.

BEYOND CHEERLEADING: WHAT REAL ENCOURAGEMENT ACTUALLY LOOKS LIKE

When most people hear "vision-driven encourager," they might picture someone with pom-poms or someone giving rah-rah speeches. That's not what we're talking about here. Real encouragement is far more sophisticated—and far more powerful.

Encouragement isn't telling someone they can do anything; it's helping them see what they're uniquely positioned to do and why it matters. It's the difference between empty cheerleading and purposeful coaching that moves the needle.

The research backs this up beautifully. Studies show that teams with leaders who consistently connect daily work to a meaningful vision demonstrate 73 percent higher engagement and 12 percent greater profitability than those without this connection. These leaders aren't just more optimistic—they're more strategic. They understand that sustainable competitive advantage doesn't come from crushing competitors, but from unleashing their team's full potential.

Vision-driven encouragers operate from a fundamental belief that every person, every team, and every challenge contains untapped potential.

Their superpower isn't unquestioning optimism—it's the vision to see possibilities that others miss and then create a transparent bridge from here to there.

In today's hyper-competitive environment, this kind of leadership isn't just nice to have—it's essential. When the pressure is on and the path forward isn't clear, people need someone who can light the way without losing their humanity. Research from Harvard Business School shows that teams led by encouraging leaders are 31 percent more productive, have 37 percent better sales performance, and are three times more likely to be engaged at work.

THE INNER FOUNDATION: YOU CAN'T GIVE WHAT YOU DON'T HAVE

Here's something most leadership books won't tell you: before you can inspire others with vision, you must first cultivate that vision within yourself. Before you can encourage others to hope, you must nurture genuine hope in your own heart.

People have incredibly sensitive radar for authenticity. They can sense within moments whether your vision comes from deep conviction or surface-level optimism. They know if your encouragement flows from genuine belief or performance pressure. The difference between inspiring leadership and empty cheerleading starts with what's happening inside you.

Cultivating Your Inner Vision

Real vision begins in solitude, not in boardrooms. It starts with those quiet moments when you ask yourself the hard questions: What do I really believe is possible? What am I genuinely excited to build? What future am I willing to work toward even when others don't see it yet?

Research from the University of Rochester found that leaders who spend time visualizing their goals with vivid emotion and detail are 42 percent more likely to achieve them. This isn't just daydreaming—it's what psychologists call "implementation intention," and it works by programming your subconscious mind to recognize opportunities and take actions aligned with your vision.

Your inner vision should be so compelling that it pulls you forward even when no one else believes it yet. If you don't feel that gravitational pull toward your vision, neither will your team.

Building Authentic Hope

Hope, like vision, must be genuine to be powerful. True hope goes beyond blind optimism; it is the strong belief that real progress can be made, even if the way forward isn't obvious.

The research on hope is remarkable. Dr. Shane Lopez's groundbreaking work found that people with higher hope scores are more successful, healthier, and happier. Moreover, hope is not merely an emotion; it is a skill that can be developed and has a measurable effect on performance. Studies from the University of Kansas found that employees with higher hope are 14 percent more productive and have 10 percent higher engagement scores than their colleagues. Charles Snyder found that hope comes down to three key components:

- Goals (knowing what you want)
- Pathways (finding ways to get there)
- Agency (believing you can do it)

When leaders cultivate all three internally, they become exponentially more effective at inspiring others.

I've learned that hope is built through a simple but profound practice—collecting evidence. Look for minor signs that your vision is taking root. Document moments when your team exceeded their own expectations. Notice incremental progress that others might miss. Keep notes or even write a hope journal if you'd like—a running record of progress, breakthrough moments, and evidence that your vision is becoming reality.

Next, once you see evidence of hope emerging, then identify the progress with your team. Research from Harvard Medical School shows that people who regularly practice gratitude and hope-building exercises show measurable improvements in optimism, life satisfaction, and resilience within just eight weeks. When you consistently look for and celebrate progress, you're not just being positive—you're literally rewiring your brain to see possibilities.

But here's the crucial part for leaders: your internal hope becomes contagious. Studies from the University of Pennsylvania demonstrate that a leader's level of hope directly predicts their team's performance, with high-hope leaders seeing 21 percent better results and 40 percent lower turnover. Your team is constantly reading your emotional state and adjusting their own expectations accordingly. When your hope is genuine and grounded in evidence, it becomes a powerful force that elevates everyone around you.

THE INTERNAL KEYS TO BECOMING A VISION-DRIVEN ENCOURAGER

See the Future First

Before you can inspire anyone else, you need to see something worth inspiring them toward—and you need to see it with crystal clarity. The most powerful visions share three characteristics:

- ambitious enough to stretch people
- relevant enough to matter to them personally
- anchored in values that won't shift when the going gets tough

Can you close your eyes and walk through your vision, as if you're giving a tour? Can you describe not just what will be different, but how it will feel when you get there? MIT research shows that leaders who can articulate their vision in sensory detail are 67 percent more likely to inspire action in others.

Turn Purpose into Participation

Here's a truth most leaders miss: people don't commit to your vision, they commit to their role in making it happen. The magic happens when you connect the big picture to the daily work each person does.

Research from Deloitte found that purpose-driven companies achieve higher market-share gains and grow, on average, three times faster than their competitors. But purpose isn't just about having a mission statement—it's about helping every team member see their work as essential to something bigger than themselves.

Everyone on your team should be able to draw a straight line from their daily tasks to the larger purpose you're pursuing. When people see their work as essential to something meaningful, everything changes.

Encourage With Surgical Precision

Generic praise falls flat. Powerful encouragement is specific—it connects a person's effort directly to the mission's progress. Instead of the nicety of "Great job," try "The way you handled that client call perfectly embodies our commitment to excellence, and it's exactly why we're going to achieve our goal."

Studies from the University of Pennsylvania show that specific, meaningful recognition increases performance by 14 percent and reduces turnover by 31 percent. Recognition becomes rocket fuel when it's tied to purpose. This where Competitive Kindness is better than just being nice.

Model Hope in Action

Vision-driven encouragers don't ignore problems—they reframe them as opportunities. People watch how you handle pressure—not just for leadership cues, but also for authenticity cues. They're asking: Does this person really believe what they're saying?

When challenges arise, asking "What can this lead to if we respond the right way?" with genuine conviction rather than forced optimism makes all the difference. Research from the University of Michigan found that leaders who model optimistic thinking during setbacks see 23 percent better team performance and 18 percent higher employee satisfaction.

WHEN VISION MATTERS MOST

Your role as a vision-driven encourager becomes most critical during four key moments:

- **Uncertainty**—When the path forward isn't clear, people need someone who can see through the fog.
- **Transitions**—When old ways are ending and new ones haven't yet formed, vision creates meaning in the middle.
- **Setbacks**—When performance dips, morale follows. Leaders must lift both simultaneously.
- **Burnout**—When effort feels thankless, vision reminds people why their work matters.

These are the moments that separate good leaders from great ones. Anyone can lead when things are going well. Vision-driven encouragers shine when the light seems dim.

THE SCIENCE OF INSPIRATION

Research strongly supports what the best leaders have always known intuitively—inspiration matters. Gallup's research shows that teams led by managers who consistently inspire enthusiasm about the future demonstrate 2.3 times higher engagement, 18 percent higher productivity, and 12 percent better customer metrics.

Dr. Kim Cameron's studies on positive leadership revealed that organizations with leaders who elevate others through vision and encouragement consistently outperform their competitors by 35 percent, especially during tough times. Even neuroscience backs this up—when people connect their work to a meaningful vision, it activates brain regions that fuel perseverance, creativity, and resilience.

The bottom line: people don't just perform better when they believe their work matters—they become better. This is where Competitive Kindness shows its true power. Traditional competitive approaches might extract short-term performance through fear or pressure, but vision-driven encouragement creates sustained excellence through inspiration and purpose.

YOUR VISION-DRIVEN LEADERSHIP TOOLKIT

Ready to put this into practice? Here are four tools you can start using immediately:

1. The Monday Vision Moment

Start each week by connecting current work to future impact. Spend five minutes reminding your team where you're going and why their work matters.

2. The "I See You" Practice

Write specific notes that say, "I saw what you did. Here's why it mattered." Keep it personal and purpose-connected.

3. The Possibility Question

When problems arise, ask your team, "What could this lead to if we handle it the right way?" Train them to see challenges as opportunities.

4. The Future-Back Planning

Start planning sessions by describing success, then work backward to identify the steps needed to get there.

THE LEADERSHIP OF POSSIBILITY

In a world filled with cynicism, pressure, and constant change, the leaders who truly make a difference are those who choose to lead with vision and encouragement. They don't just manage what is—they mobilize what could be.

This is the essence of Competitive Kindness: competing with such vision and encouragement that you don't just win—you elevate everyone around you in the process. These leaders understand that their job isn't just to hit targets or solve problems—it's to help people see more in themselves, more in the mission, and more in the moment than they could see on their own.

They prove that you can be relentlessly committed to excellence while being genuinely committed to people. They show that the most powerful competitive advantage isn't beating others down—it's lifting your team so high that the competition can't reach you.

Vision-driven encouragers believe in a better future, then help others feel it too. And in doing so, they don't just build high-performing teams. They create lasting legacies that change industries, communities, and lives.

The question isn't whether you have a vision. The question is whether your vision is compelling enough to inspire others to pick up a brush and help you paint the masterpiece, while becoming masterpieces themselves in the process.

CHAPTER 12

EMPOWER INDIVIDUAL WORTH

> The competitively kind leaders don't just see teammates—they see human beings with dreams, struggles, strengths, and stories that extend far beyond the workplace.
>
> *"Leadership is not about being in charge.*
> *It's about taking care of those in your charge."*
> Simon Sinek

CASE STUDY: BASEBALL, THE WHOLE BRAIN, AND NATIONAL ACCLAIM

As the umpire called strike three, my first season at a once-storied baseball university came to an incredibly quiet ending. The few hundred people in the stands enjoyed the California sun, but the atmosphere was severely lacking. Our once-proud program was playing to half-empty stands, lost in a crowded media market where professional teams dominated the sports landscape. Revenues were abysmal. Something had to change.

My first instinct? Launch a traditional marketing blitz. Cut ticket prices. Reorganize our promotional staff. After all, empty seats kill momentum, and momentum drives championship programs. But something stopped me cold. Instead of scheduling another strategy meeting, I asked a mentor for guidance, and he challenged me to ask a completely different question: *"What if we're thinking about this all wrong?"*

That simple shift in perspective changed everything—not just for our baseball program, but for how I understood what it means to truly empower the diverse minds around us to create something extraordinary.

The Mind Behind the Mission

Here's what I discovered when I started really listening to the different people in our organization—not as job titles delivering reports, but as unique human beings with distinct ways of thinking: everyone saw the solution differently, and they were all right.

- Our data-driven ticket operations director lived and breathed attendance figures, demographic studies, and revenue projections.
- Our ticket sales director thought in terms of relationships, emotional connections, and the human stories that make people fall in love with a team.
- Our event operations manager focused on logistics, detailed planning, and creating reliable system.
- Our marketing director was craving to fill the stands with an electric atmosphere that would make any television network salivate.

Each was frustrated because they felt their approach wasn't being heard or valued. We weren't dealing with a marketing problem—we were dealing with a fundamental disconnect between how different minds naturally approached the same challenge.

THE FOUR MINDS OF CHAMPIONSHIP BUILDING

My mentor's question led me to the power of thinking differently through a different model. Ned Herrmann's Whole Brain® Thinking model, developed through extensive neurological research, reveals that people process information through four distinct thinking approaches:

1. THE ANALYTICAL MIND: Lives for data, metrics, ROI analysis, and systematic evaluation of what works
2. THE ORGANIZED MIND: Thrives on detailed planning, operational systems, and step-by-step execution
3. THE INTERPERSONAL MIND: Focuses on relationships, community connections, and emotional engagement
4. THE CREATIVE MIND: Sees innovative possibilities, breakthrough ideas, and unconventional solutions

COGNITIVE STYLE LEADERSHIP FRAMEWORK

QUADRANT	HOW THEY PROCESS	WHAT THEY NEED	HOW TO SUPPORT THEM
ANALYTICAL	Logic, facts, data	Clear expectations, measurable goals	Provide context, share rationale, celebrate data-driven wins
ORGANIZED	Structure, process, details	Consistent systems, clear timelines	Create reliable routines, acknowledge thoroughness, provide stability
INTERPERSONAL	Relationships, emotions, values	Connection, psychological safety	Check in personally, recognize their impact on others, create team bonding
CREATIVE	Possibilities, innovation, big picture	Creative freedom, future vision	Share the bigger purpose, encourage experimentation, celebrate innovation

Here's the game-changing insight: our baseball revival required all four thinking approaches working in harmony. The leaders who master Competitive Kindness understand that empowering individual worth means recognizing and strategically leveraging these different mental approaches to create something no one could achieve alone.

Learning from the Pros: A Strategic Discovery Mission

We arranged a visit to a local professional baseball team for all of us to understand their success in the crowded marketplace. What we discovered wasn't a single strategy—it was a sophisticated operation leveraging every type of thinking.

- Their analytics team had identified precise demographic targets and pricing strategies based on exhaustive data analysis.
- Their operations crew had created seamless systems for group sales, parking, and fan experience management.
- Their community relations staff had built deep relationships with local organizations and schools.
- Their marketing creatives had developed innovative promotional concepts that captured imagination and generated buzz.

As our eyes were opened to their diverse approaches, we had a breakthrough. This team wasn't just selling baseball—they were creating an integrated experience that appealed to different types of people through different cognitive approaches.

THE FOUR PATHWAYS TO COMPETITIVE KINDNESS IN ACTION

Supporting the Analytical Mind

Marcus, our ticket operations director, was drowning in data but felt like nobody listened to his insights. When I started speaking his language—numbers, trends, measurable outcomes—something magical happened. His confidence soared. His presentations became compelling. For the first time, he felt truly valued for his analytical brilliance.

Marcus dove deep into attendance patterns, demographic analysis, and revenue optimization models. He identified that our biggest opportunity wasn't attracting individual fans—it was capturing local groups that could fill sections at a time. His data showed group sales generated significantly more revenue per fan and created the energetic atmosphere that made games exciting for everyone.

Analytical Mind Leadership Through Competitive Kindness

Here are some observations that can assist you as you engage with the team member who operates with the Analytical Mind:

- Provide comprehensive data and market research—meet them in their language of evidence
- Create measurable frameworks for tracking success—give them the metrics they need to excel
- Allow time for thorough analysis before expecting recommendations—honor their systematic approach
- Partner with relationship-builders who can execute their insights—create cognitive complementarity
- Celebrate their contributions to strategic decision-making—affirm their unique analytical value

The Competitive Kindness advantage: When analytical minds feel understood and valued for their data-driven insights, they become strategic powerhouses who identify breakthrough opportunities and provide the rigorous foundation that makes bold initiatives successful.

Supporting the Organized Mind

Jennifer, our event operations manager, was naturally gifted at creating systems and managing complex logistics, but she felt overwhelmed by our ambitious attendance goals and worried about operational chaos if we succeeded in filling the stadium.

The Competitive Kindness breakthrough came when I stopped seeing her concerns as obstacles and started seeing them as operational genius. Instead of asking her to "just figure it out," we channeled her organizational brilliance into creating "scalable excellence"—detailed systems for group sales processing, coordinated parking and concession flows, and comprehensive game-day procedures.

Jennifer became our operational architect. Her systematic approach to handling large crowds became our competitive advantage. When you help organized minds become the best version of themselves, they don't just prevent problems—they create reliable excellence that allows big dreams to become sustainable reality.

Organized Mind Leadership Through Competitive Kindness

Here are some observations that can assist you as you engage with the team member who operates with the Organized Mind:

- Provide detailed planning timelines and operational frameworks—give them the structure they need to excel
- Create comprehensive playbooks for managing complex logistics—leverage their natural organizational gifts
- Recognize their contributions to seamless execution—celebrate their behind-the-scenes excellence
- Give them lead time to prepare for major initiatives—respect their need for thorough planning
- Support their systematic approach with adequate resources—honor their commitment to operational excellence

The Competitive Kindness advantage: When organized minds feel valued for their systematic approach, they become operational powerhouses who turn ambitious visions into seamless reality and create the reliable foundations that allow breakthrough success to be sustained and scaled.

Supporting the Interpersonal Mind

Miguel, our ticket sales director, had incredible instincts for building relationships and understanding what motivated different groups, but he felt like his interpersonal approach wasn't valued in our data-driven environment.

The moment we honored his relationship-building strengths while providing analytical support, everything changed. We paired him with Marcus, who could provide data insights that supported his intuitive understanding of community dynamics. More importantly, we positioned his interpersonal gifts as the critical bridge between our analytical insights and actual results.

Miguel became our community engagement superstar. He built relationships with youth leagues, corporate groups, junior high academies, alumni organizations, and civic clubs. His ability to understand what different groups valued and how to make them feel genuinely welcome became the emotional foundation of our attendance revolution.

Interpersonal Mind Leadership Through Competitive Kindness

Here are some observations that can assist you as you engage with the team member who operates with the Interpersonal Mind:

- Create opportunities for relationship building with diverse community groups—feed their natural energy source
- Value their intuitive understanding of what motivates different people—appreciate their emotional intelligence
- Provide analytical support that enhances rather than replaces their relational approach—honor their human-centered perspective
- Recognize their contributions to community engagement and fan loyalty—celebrate their relationship-building impact
- Give them space to build consensus and create authentic connections—respect their collaborative nature

The Competitive Kindness advantage: When interpersonal minds feel appreciated for their relationship-building gifts, they become community engagement powerhouses who create the authentic connections and emotional loyalty that transform casual attendees into passionate, long-term supporters. This leads to capturing the hearts and minds of many constituents.

Supporting the Creative Mind

Kim, our marketing director, was constantly generating innovative promotional ideas and seeing possibilities others missed. But budget constraints and traditional approaches were systematically crushing her creative spirit, turning our greatest source of breakthrough thinking into a frustrated rule-follower.

The Competitive Kindness transformation happened when we created "innovation labs" within our structured planning process—dedicated brainstorming sessions, experimental promotional concepts, and permission to try unconventional approaches. We positioned these creative explorations as essential to our competitive advantage, not indulgent departures from "real work."

Kim's creative mind revolutionized our entire approach to fan engagement. She developed themed game experiences, innovative group packages, and social media campaigns that captured imagination and generated buzz throughout our media market.

Creative Mind Leadership Through Competitive Kindness

Here are some observations that can assist you as you engage with the team member who operates with the Creative Mind:

- Provide unstructured time for creative exploration and innovative thinking—honor their need for mental freedom
- Encourage cross-functional collaboration with diverse team members—fuel their innovative connections
- Allow for experimental approaches and iterative learning—embrace their trial-and-discovery process
- Recognize their contributions to innovative fan engagement and market differentiation—celebrate their future-focused thinking
- Create spaces for big-picture visioning alongside detailed execution planning—balance creativity with implementation

The Competitive Kindness advantage: When creative minds feel valued for their visionary gifts, they become innovative engines that drive breakthrough thinking, challenge conventional approaches, and create the forward-looking solutions that establish lasting competitive differentiation.

THE COMPETITIVE ADVANTAGE
OF WHOLE-MIND LEADERSHIP

While most organizations exhaust themselves trying to fix weaknesses or force everyone to think the same way, leading with Competitive Kindness amplifies people's cognitive strengths while providing strategic support for their growth areas. The result isn't just better performance—it's organizational transformation that creates sustainable competitive advantage.

FOUR KEY ADVANTAGES OF COGNITIVE DIVERSITY

1. Cognitive Diversity Drives Breakthrough Solutions

Teams with all four thinking approaches represented are 70 percent more likely to develop breakthrough strategies. When Marcus's analytical insights met Kim's creative vision, supported by Jennifer's operational excellence and Miguel's community relationships, we didn't just get better attendance—we created a fan experience no one could have achieved alone.

2. Reduced Mental Exhaustion Unleashes Hidden Potential

Research from neuroscientist Dr. Arlene Taylor reveals that when we're forced to operate primarily outside our natural thinking preferences, our brains consume 100 times more glucose—literally exhausting us. When people operate primarily in their natural thinking style, they have exponentially more mental energy for complex problem-solving and resilient performance under pressure.

3. Enhanced Psychological Safety Creates Fearless Innovation

When team members understand that different thinking approaches are valuable competitive assets, psychological safety skyrockets. Marcus stopped apologizing for asking tough analytical questions and started driving rigorous strategic thinking. Kim stopped feeling constrained by conventional approaches and started contributing visionary innovations.

4. Collective Genius Through Individual Excellence

When each person operates from their zone of cognitive genius, the collective capability of the team multiplies exponentially. You're not just managing different personalities—you're orchestrating complementary forms of intelligence to create results that redefine what's possible.

THE CHAMPIONSHIP RESULTS: WHEN COMPETITIVE KINDNESS WINS

The transformation was extraordinary. Within two seasons of implementing whole-mind leadership through Competitive Kindness, our baseball program experienced a complete revival:

- **Marcus's analytical insights** identified group sales strategies that consistently filled our stadium.
- **Jennifer's operational excellence** created seamless game-day experiences that made our historic venue legendary for fan satisfaction.
- **Miguel's relationship-building genius** generated community connections that filled entire sections with passionate, engaged fans.
- **Kim's creative innovations** generated buzz throughout our media market and created unique fan experiences.

On one Tuesday evening game, legendary baseball broadcaster Dick Enberg was in attendance in the press box. He asked me, why there were so many people at the game when the opponent was considered lackluster. I looked at my phone to see the marketing schedule and said, "It's Harry Potter Night! There are several hundred fan clubs and some college Quidditch teams competing on the field after the game." The legend spoke a powerful truth in response, "Well, you have something special brewing here."

The team's performance started to match the energy of the crowds. This led to a conference championship and a perfect 9-0 record on Friday

Night Fireworks games. When the team reached the NCAA Regionals and Super Regionals, we were selected as one of the host sites. This was the first time in nearly twenty years that the university was selected as a host venue for the postseason. The ballpark was electric! After winning the NCAA Regionals and falling just short of advancing to the College Baseball World Series, we were reflecting on the success of the season. Just then, I received text messages from several ESPN executives telling me that this was the most thrilling and loudest venue they'd experienced in college baseball that season—even though our stadium was smaller than several schools in the highly-touted Southeastern Conference (SEC).

More importantly, we had created a sustainable culture of excellence where people brought their best cognitive selves to work every day. That's how Competitive Kindness creates championship organizations: one unleashed mind at a time.

THE SCIENCE BEHIND HIGH-PERFORMANCE TEAMS

Not only are you valuing individual worth by allowing your teammates to be themselves. Research supports the dramatic impact of leveraging individual thinking preferences:

- **Cognitive efficiency increases by 40%** when people operate in their natural thinking style
- **Team problem-solving improves by 60%** when all four thinking approaches are represented
- **Team engagement scores increase by 35%** when leaders adapt their approach to individual thinking preferences
- **Stress-related turnover decreases by 45%** when role demands align with cognitive strengths
- **Breakthrough innovation increases by 300%** when creative minds are properly supported and integrated

The Mind-Aware Leadership Framework

Instead of generic performance conversations, try this thinking-style-aware approach. Unleash the power of your team members and accentuate their individual worth by asking questions that align with their thinking strengths.

FOR ANALYTICAL MINDS:

- "What data would help you identify our biggest opportunities?"
- "Where do you need more analytical clarity to drive results?"
- "What measurable frameworks would support your success?"

FOR ORGANIZED MINDS:

- "What systems would make our operations more efficient and reliable?"
- "Where do you need more structure or planning time to excel?"
- "What logistical details are keeping you concerned about our success?"

FOR INTERPERSONAL MINDS:

- "What relationship opportunities are we missing in our community?"
- "How can we better connect with the groups that matter most?"
- "Where do you need more support for building authentic relationships?"

FOR CREATIVE MINDS:

- "What innovative possibilities are you excited about exploring?"
- "Where do you need more creative freedom to generate breakthrough ideas?"
- "What big-picture vision is driving your most innovative thinking?"

A Suggested Implementation Framework

WEEK 1: THINKING STYLE DISCOVERY

Help each team member to identify their natural thinking preferences. This can be accomplished by asking questions like:

- "When facing a complex challenge, what's your first instinct?"
- "What energizes you most in your role?"
- "What drains your energy fastest?"

WEEK 2-3: ROLE ALIGNMENT CONVERSATIONS

In order to effectively create alignment for each individual on the team, it is critical for each person, explore the connection between their natural thinking preferences and their existing role on the team. Such questions they should answer include:

- "Where does your role leverage your natural thinking strengths?"
- "Where does your role require thinking approaches that drain your energy?"
- "How can we restructure responsibilities to play to cognitive strengths?"
- "Who could complement your thinking style on key initiatives?"

WEEK 4: TEAM INTEGRATION STRATEGY

This step can be complex and may require more than just you thinking this through. Ask your team to help you map out the team's collective thinking profile:

- "Where are your cognitive strengths as an organization?"
- "What thinking approaches are underrepresented?"
- "How can you structure meetings and projects to leverage all thinking styles?"
- "What strategic partnerships would create more balanced cognitive teams?"

IDENTIFYING YOUR PERSONAL LEADERSHIP BIAS

Understanding your own thinking preferences is crucial for empowering others effectively. It is also important to understand that your thinking preference may have innate bias towards other thinking preferences or simply might cause you agitation. To integrate this model in your leadership, you must self-assess to identify your biases. Don't feel bad. Everyone has biases.

To conduct this self-assessment, try asking yourself questions like:

- "What thinking style energizes you most under pressure?"
- "Which thinking style do you find most challenging to understand during tight deadlines?"
- "How does your thinking preference influence who you rely on, promote, or find frustrating?"
- "What cognitive blind spots might you have in your leadership during high-stakes situations?"

Once you have identified your leadership bias, it is essential that you continually self-check so that you can empower all of your team to work within their natural thinking preference and drive trust.

YOUR WHOLE-MIND LEADERSHIP CHALLENGE

This week, identify one person on your team whose thinking style is most different from yours. Instead of trying to change how they think, get curious about how their mind works. Find out some of these things:

- What do they see that you miss during challenging situations?
- How do they process complex information differently than you do?
- What strengths do they bring that complement your own?
- How could you restructure their role to leverage their natural thinking style for maximum impact?

Then have a conversation with them about their cognitive preferences. Ask what energizes them, what drains them, and how they'd like to contribute during critical moments. Listen not just to what they say, but to how they think. Your eyes will open and new possibilities to thrive will emerge.

THE FUTURE OF LEADERSHIP THROUGH COMPETITIVE KINDNESS

The ultimate competitive advantage lies in our ability to unleash human cognitive diversity through Competitive Kindness. The leaders who will dominate the future are those who understand that empowering individual worth means empowering individual minds to become their absolute best.

Competitive Kindness isn't about being nice to people despite their differences—it's about being strategically brilliant enough to leverage those cognitive differences for championship results. It's about recognizing that the analytical mind, the organized mind, the interpersonal heart, and the creative spirit aren't competing approaches—they're complementary forms of genius that, when properly honored and integrated, can solve any challenge and create any level of success.

When we lead through Competitive Kindness this way, we don't just empower individual worth—we unleash collective genius that transforms organizations and entire communities. In that transformation, everyone doesn't just win—they become the best version of themselves while creating something extraordinary together.

The question isn't whether people think differently—neuroscience has definitively settled that debate. The question is whether you're ready to leverage those differences through Competitive Kindness to help people become the best version of themselves while creating championship-level results together.

That's the power of whole-mind leadership through Competitive Kindness. That's how you empower individual worth by unleashing individual genius. That's how you create winning organizations by helping everyone win as the best version of themselves. That's how a struggling baseball program becomes the loudest, most thrilling venue in the country—one empowered mind at a time.

CHAPTER 13

ELEVATE OTHERS THROUGH SERVICE

Leading with Competitive Kindness positions others to reach heights they never thought possible. When we serve with the intent of elevating, we don't just create followers, we create future leaders who will carry forward a legacy of excellence.

"When we are kind, we help others to trust themselves, to believe in their worth, and to discover possibilities they may not have seen before."
Piero Ferrucci, The Power of Kindness

THE ANNIHILATED KNEE, ICE CREAM, AND THE POWER OF ELEVATION

I was running down the sideline as the lead blocker for our speedy running back. Only a few weeks earlier, I was listed in the local newspaper and by local television sports anchors as one of the top high school recruits in the state—receiving letters and calls from some of the top Division I football schools in the country. In fact, several coaches in the stands were evaluating my performance in that game. I was leading the state in sacks as a defensive end and had just made an "incredible" one-handed catch as a tight end against the team touted as the championship favorite.

Back to running down the sideline. During one offensive play, I ran ahead of our running back and planted my right foot to make a block behind me and to my left. Just as I planted my foot, a player from the other team dove with the crown of his helmet directly at my knee. It was intentional. It was devastating. The doctors indicated that I would never play football again. In fact, the injury I sustained was so severe that another doctor later told me that had I torn one more ligament, my lower leg would have needed to be amputated.

With my dreams crushed after the first of several surgeries, I lay in bed hooked up to a machine designed to constantly bend my knee to prevent my tendons from shortening and blood clots from forming. My teenage mind was trying to comprehend the enormous changes happening before me, and a whole new reality was setting in. I didn't know it yet, but a simple gesture was about to become one of the most profound leadership lessons I have ever experienced.

There was a knock on my bedroom door. Wiping the tears from my eyes, I tried to prepare myself for a visitor. Several kind people had stopped by to share their support, but this visit was different. It was my former bishop from my church congregation, and he had brought me my favorite ice cream. As he walked in, he said, "I know that ice cream helps me feel better when I have a big task to accomplish." I was a little confused but very grateful because food didn't sit well, but ice cream always hits the spot. He leaned in, "Hopefully, this ice cream can be the start of your big comeback!"

Before that moment, I was just trying to relearn the basics of showering, using the bathroom, and not passing out when I was upright on crutches for more than a minute. And here he was talking about my comeback! Not only did his kind gesture of ice cream lighten the mood through his serving heart, but his words of faith and encouragement literally lifted my soul to get back out onto the football field. Despite many naysayers throughout the next year, including an antagonistic physical therapist—I was back on the football field the following season, enroute to earning a college football scholarship. That brief visit from my former bishop demonstrated to me that when you serve to elevate others, you can inspire people to achieve the seemingly impossible.

THE SCIENCE OF ELEVATING OTHERS

The most compelling evidence for service-oriented leadership comes from decades of research showing that leaders who focus on elevating others create measurably superior outcomes. Studies demonstrate that servant leadership, which emphasizes mutual exchange of concern and care between leaders and team members, translates into positive work outcomes, including enhanced performance and organizational citizenship behaviors. Servant leadership positively influences employee engagement through various mediators, including empowerment, team cohesion, a favorable organizational climate, challenging tasks, and proactive personality development. It isn't just about making people feel good—it's about creating conditions where human potential can flourish. Most importantly, comprehensive research indicates that servant leadership behaviors have a significant organizational impact. Servant leadership predicted an additional 19 percent variance in community citizenship behaviors and 5 percent variance in in-role performance, demonstrating measurable returns on investment in people development. The research is clear: servant leadership is essential to individual and organizational excellence.

So, to develop people and elevate their thinking, there are four key components of servant leadership within the context of Competitive Kindness:

1. Measure What Matters: The Development Dividend

The most successful leaders understand that traditional metrics—revenue, titles, recognition—are lagging indicators. The leading indicator of sustainable success is the number of people you've helped reach their next level of capability and contribution. Competitively kind servant leaders enhance a sense of meaningfulness, which strengthens the effectiveness of leadership behaviors and leads to increased empowerment, improved well-being, and ultimately the experience of flow. When people feel their growth matters to their leader, they invest more deeply in both their own development and the organization's success.

I learned this from a mentor who kept what he called his "Elevation Inventory." Every quarter, he would ask himself:

- Who grew because of our work together?
- What barriers did I help someone break through?
- Which person is now equipped to help others the way I helped them?

This practice transformed how he viewed his role—not as the person who had all the answers, but as the person who helped others discover their own answers.

Your Turn: This week, start your own Elevation Inventory. Identify three people you're actively developing right now. Document the specific growth you're seeing and how their progress creates value that extends beyond just them. Track these development wins with the same intensity you track business metrics.

2. Listen with Elevation Intent

Sadly, most conversations are transactional—we listen to gather information or wait for our turn to speak. When you listen with elevation intent, you're listening for potential, possibility, and breakthrough moments. You're studying the person in front of you like a coach studies game film, seeking to understand how to unlock their next level of performance.

Spears identified listening as one of the ten fundamental characteristics of servant leadership, noting that leaders have traditionally been valued for their communication and decision-making skills. Still, these must be reinforced by a deep commitment to listening intently to others. This research demonstrates that competitively kind servant leaders who master strategic listening create environments where integrity, altruism, humility, empathy and healing, personal growth focus, fairness and justice, and empowerment flourish.

Over the years, I've developed "Elevation Conversations" with my team. Instead of status updates or performance reviews, these are strategic sessions focused on accelerating their path to excellence. I ask three core questions:

- "What's currently working well that we can amplify?"
- "What's the one barrier that, if removed, would change everything for you?"
- "What resources or support would help you reach your goals twice as fast?"

Here's what happens next: powerful silence. People aren't used to someone genuinely wanting to accelerate their success. But in that pause, they start thinking differently about their challenges and possibilities. This isn't just good relationship building—it's a strategic intelligence gathering that transforms both individual performance and collective results.

3. Elevate Through Accountability

Here's where competitively kind, service-oriented leadership faces its ultimate test: when someone needs honest feedback about their performance. This is the moment that separates Competitive Kindness leaders who elevate from merely nice people-pleasers.

The key insight is this: you can deliver the most brutal truths while preserving human dignity and potential. In fact, you *must*. When you attack someone's character or competence, you're not just giving feedback—you're damaging the very person you need to perform better. But when you focus on specific behaviors and outcomes while affirming their worth and potential, you create the psychological safety necessary for real change.

So, how can you elevate through competitively kind correction? Here are several suggestions rooted in research that form an "elevation-focused correction framework:"

SEPARATE THE PERSON FROM THE PERFORMANCE: Start with an affirmation of their value to the organization, what your team needs from them to reach their potential, and then address the specific issue. "You're a crucial part of this team that needs you to close the sale, AND we need to talk about what happened yesterday."

FOCUS ON IMPACT, NOT INTENT: Don't guess why they did something. Stick to observable behaviors and measurable outcomes. "When you miss deadlines, it creates a bottleneck for the entire project and our processes for success," rather than "You're irresponsible." Adding labels to people rather than focusing on performance impact will inevitably lead to Competitive Cruelty.

BE SPECIFIC ABOUT THE PATH FORWARD: Vague feedback creates anxiety. Clear direction creates confidence. Instead of "You need to do better," try "Here are the three specific things that need to change… and here's how we'll measure the progress toward success…"

REINFORCE YOUR INVESTMENT IN THEIR SUCCESS: End every difficult conversation by reaffirming your belief in their potential. "We're having this conversation because I know you're capable of more. Our team needs you to thrive to win. I'm committed to helping you take the next step."

FOLLOW THROUGH WITH SUPPORT: Don't just identify problems—become part of the solution. "What obstacles are preventing you from succeeding, and how can I help remove them?"

This isn't about being soft—it's about being strategically brilliant and competitively kind. When you preserve someone's dignity while addressing their performance, you tap into their intrinsic desire to build the team and prove you right rather than their urge to prove you wrong.

4. Create a Multiplication Effect Through Servant Leadership

Traditional leadership thinking operates from scarcity—the belief that there's only so much success to go around. True, competitively kind leaders leverage servant leadership to flip this paradigm by embracing an abundance mindset rooted in service to others. When we lead by elevating those around us, we don't diminish our own impact—we multiply it exponentially through the lives we transform.

The real magic happens in the "Service Multiplication Effect." When those you serve and elevate become servant leaders themselves, you create an ever-expanding circle of impact that extends far beyond your immediate sphere. Studies found that leaders with a servant mindset enhance followers' adaptability and proactivity while developing positive job attitudes. In other words, you can influence the people you lead to become servant leaders themselves.

This process of elevating servant leaders around you is intentional and can follow a four-step process for each person on your team:

1. STRETCH THROUGH SERVICE: Where can they take on bigger challenges that not only develop their capabilities but also serve a greater purpose?
2. OWNERSHIP THROUGH IMPACT: What meaningful victories can they own that make a real difference for others?
3. LEADING BY SERVING: How are they developing and serving others in their sphere of influence?
4. AMPLIFYING THEIR SERVICE: What opportunities exist for them to showcase how their growth enables them to serve at higher levels?

The goal isn't to create dependency, but to elevate team members to become independent servant leaders. In fact, you are creating a team of leaders. Your effectiveness isn't measured by how indispensable you are, but by how many capable, caring leaders you develop who go on to elevate others. It is leadership through service—where your most significant achievement is not what you accomplish, but what you enable others to achieve for the benefit of all.

WHEN ELEVATION THROUGH SERVICE BECOMES YOUR STRATEGIC ADVANTAGE

There are specific situations where Competitive Kindness drives teams to thrive through genuine care for the team. And also, because it's smart strategy. Here are a few of these critical situations:

During Crisis

When everything's falling apart, elevating leaders don't look for scapegoats; they look for ways to bring out the best in their people under pressure. They step into the challenge with their team, not above it.

In High-Stakes Environments

When pressure is maximum and stakes are high, service-minded leaders remain focused on collective excellence. This stability becomes rocket fuel for unified team performance when others are operating from fear.

During Transformation

When you're trying to change the game entirely, elevating others creates a shared sense of purpose that makes breakthrough results possible. People will follow you through uncertainty when they trust you're invested in their success.

THE LONG GAME OF ELEVATING OTHERS

Here's the truth about serving to elevate others: it's not the fastest path to individual recognition, but it's the most sustainable path to meaningful impact. It's not about being soft—it's about being strategically brilliant. Service leadership is Competitive Kindness in its purest form.

When you elevate others through service, you're wielding a competitive weapon that transforms entire ecosystems. Research demonstrates that servant leadership reduces turnover and creates psychological safety. In a world where talent is mobile and loyalty is rare, those who elevate others create genuine competitive advantage through collective excellence.

This is where Competitive Kindness reveals its ultimate strategic power. While others compete for zero-sum victories, you're expanding the entire playing field. You're not just winning—you're changing the game itself.

To serve first is to lead with courage. When you use your influence to elevate others, you don't lose your edge—you gain something far more powerful: accelerated trust, multiplied talent, and sustainable impact. You create a competitive moat built on abundance, not scarcity.

The leaders who master this understand that Competitive Kindness isn't about being nice—it's about being necessary. When you consistently elevate others, you become irreplaceable not through hoarding opportunities, but through creating them.

The question isn't whether you're generous enough to elevate others. The question is whether you're strategic enough to recognize that Competitive Kindness—the deliberate choice to out-serve, out-develop, and out-elevate your competition—is the ultimate leadership advantage.

That's how you turn the development of others into your greatest strategic asset. That's how Competitive Kindness transforms from a philosophy into systematic advantage.

SPEAK WITH PURPOSE

> Words have immense power to transform lives and drive business results—every conversation is an opportunity to help someone see their potential through Competitive Kindness.
>
> *"Kind words can be short and easy to speak, but their echoes are truly endless."*
> Mother Teresa

THE TURNING POINT CONVERSATION

It was 2:47 p.m. on a Tuesday, and I was rushing out of my high school classroom to travel to the college football field where I coached in the evenings. I was tired and in a hurry. One of my students caught me before I headed out the door.

"Hey, Coach Clark! Do you think I should take AP History next year?"

I stopped in my tracks, looked him in the eye, and said, "Absolutely! Why wouldn't you? You'd do great. Here, let me sign that form."

Thirty seconds. Maybe less. Just another quick interaction in a day full of them.

Fast forward to the end of the school year. That same student left me a note that stopped me in my tracks. He wrote that our brief conversation saved his life. Unbeknownst to me, he had been battling thoughts of suicide, feeling worthless and directionless. That evening, he had planned to take action on his suicidal thoughts, but in that moment when I said, "Why wouldn't you?" something shifted in him. Those casual words became his lifeline—proof that someone believed in him when he couldn't believe in himself.

I sat there staring at that note, realizing the gravity of the powerful words I had just read. I immediately thought to myself, what if I hadn't responded the way I did? It became a moment of profound learning for me. Even in moments of haste, what we say really matters. In thirty seconds, I'd practiced Competitive Kindness without even knowing it—helping someone see their potential clearly while maintaining high expectations. I did not realize that psychologists call this phenomenon the "reflected appraisal theory"—the idea that we come to see ourselves primarily as we believe others see us. The powerful influence of our words makes speaking with purpose a core tenet of Competitive Kindness.

THE HIDDEN POWER OF INTENTIONAL DELIVERY

Every conversation is a choice. You can use your words as instruments of positive impact, helping people see their potential, or as weapons of criticism, leaving them wounded and defensive. The difference isn't solely in the message—it's in the delivery through Competitive Kindness.

Neuroscience research reveals why this matters so much. Studies using fMRI technology show that positive verbal feedback activates the brain's reward centers, specifically the ventral striatum, leading to *increased motivation and performance.* Conversely, harsh criticism triggers the brain's threat detection system, flooding the amygdala and limiting the brain's capacity for learning and growth. Your words literally can inspire motivation or diminish learning and growth in the brain, so be wise about your approach!

When you speak with purpose and Competitive Kindness, you're choosing to compete for people's potential while connecting hearts and minds. You're providing feedback that helps people grow rather than criticism that makes them shrink. This approach aligns with decades of research in positive psychology, which shows that strengths-based leadership significantly outperforms deficit-focused approaches across performance outcomes and employee engagement.

Think about the leaders who have influenced you the most. I'll bet they mastered this balance of Competitive Kindness. They could challenge you and encourage you in the same breath. They held high standards while speaking life into your capabilities. Research on transformational leadership confirms this intuition. Leaders who combine high expectations with individualized consideration and inspirational motivation consistently achieve superior results. You want to win— choose Competitive Kindness through intentional communication.

THREE TRUTHS ABOUT COMPETITIVE KINDNESS THROUGH WORDS

Because your words matter, here are three truths that will help you effectively build your skillset of intentional communication:

Truth #1: Words Shape Identity

When you tell someone, "You're exactly who I want leading this project," you're not just delegating a project—you're defining how they see themselves through Competitive Kindness. Social identity theory demonstrates that how we interact with significant others in our work environment essentially constructs our professional identities. Dutton also found that when leaders communicate positive regard and high expectations, employees develop more expansive and capable professional identities. So, be intentional because your words shape the identities of those you lead.

Truth #2: Words Build a Culture of Competitive Kindness Daily

Mission statements on locker room walls don't build culture. It's built through daily language rooted in Competitive Kindness. Edgar Schein's seminal work on organizational culture emphasizes that culture is primarily transmitted through leaders' daily behaviors and communications. The words that you say daily to those around you will have a greater impact on culture than any words written in a strategic plan or on the walls of your buildings. Furthermore, Goleman found that leader communication patterns account for up to 30 percent of the variance in team climate and performance. If you want culture to align with winning, Competitive Kindness will lessen the variance between your words and a winning culture.

Truth #3: Words Prove Your Authenticity

People are watching to see if your Competitive Kindness philosophy is genuine or just corporate mumbo-jumbo. Avolio & Gardner found that perceived authenticity is primarily determined by consistency between espoused values and daily behaviors, particularly in how leaders communicate with their teams. That's scholarly research demonstrating that your people can see the emptiness in your political jargon. So, practice genuine authenticity like we discussed earlier in this book. Furthermore, Gallup's extensive research demonstrates that employees who trust their manager's authenticity are twelve times more likely to be engaged at work. Once people believe you are who you say you are, then you will get buy-in. Your words drive the benefits of authentic leadership through Competitive Kindness.

FIVE STRATEGIES FOR SPEAKING WITH COMPETITIVE KINDNESS

Alright, now you see the value in your words. The natural tendency is to get nervous about what words you use, knowing your words are so powerful. So, how do you approach this so you don't have to live each day walking on eggshells?

Here are five strategies to help you on your journey to speak with power through Competitive Kindness:

1. Speak to Potential Through Competitive Kindness

Look beyond where someone is today and speak to where they're headed. Carol Dweck's groundbreaking research on growth mindset shows that when leaders focus on their teammates' potential and development rather than fixed traits, performance improves dramatically. Instead of "You're not quite there yet," try "You're closer than you think—here's how we bridge that final gap together." This approach activates what psychologists call "possible selves"—mental representations of what one might become, which are incredibly powerful motivators. This also helps people know that you genuinely care that they become the best version of themselves, which is also a critical component of Competitive Kindness.

2. Focus on Behavior with Competitive Kindness

When giving feedback, address actions rather than personal identity. Replace "You're disorganized" with "Let's work on some systems to help you stay on top of priorities." Studies have found that feedback focused on behaviors rather than personal characteristics leads to better performance outcomes and maintains psychological safety. Other research found that this behavioral focus reduces defensive responses by 40 percent while increasing implementation of feedback by 60 percent. It sounds almost too good to be true, but it's scientifically proven. If you want people to do what you ask, then be kind!

3. Create "I See in You" Moments—Competitive Kindness in Action

Make it a practice to regularly tell people what strengths and potential you see in them. Studies show that specific, strengths-based recognition increases individual performance by an average of 12 to 15 percent. Additionally, the Losada ratio research suggests that high-performing teams experience a ratio of approximately six positive interactions for every negative one. These aren't empty compliments—they're strategic observations rooted in Competitive Kindness that unlock potential. When you positively affirm strengths at a higher ratio, your team will win.

4. Honor People in Their Absence – Competitive Kindness Behind Closed Doors

How you speak about team members when they're not in the room says everything about your commitment to Competitive Kindness. Research on psychological safety shows that team members' willingness to take risks and be vulnerable directly correlates with their confidence that leaders will not embarrass or punish them. Teams with high psychological safety demonstrate 35 percent better performance and 47 percent fewer safety incidents. Backbiting and gossip is a hallmark of Competitive Cruelty. Don't do it! Ask yourself, "If they were in the room, would I say this?" If not, then cut it out and elevate your words. Being competitively kind at all times will increase confidence, effective risk-taking and innovation, and drive better performance.

5. Match Your Tone to Competitive Kindness Intent

Truth matters, but how you deliver it through Competitive Kindness might matter even more. Research in "Emotional Contagion" demonstrates that leaders' emotional tone spreads throughout their teams, influencing both morale and performance. Studies show that the same feedback delivered with different emotional tones can produce vastly different outcomes. Leaders that use supportive tones increase receptivity by up to 40 percent. This isn't about being bubbly or fake—your competitively kind tone will positively impact your team's ability to be led. Your team will match your tone, so be intentional in your tone.

THREE PRACTICAL WAYS TO SPEAK WITH PURPOSE

Let's add some practical ways that you can speak with intention and purpose in your Competitive Kindness journey:

1. Anchor Your Words in Competitive Kindness, Not Perfection

You don't need to be perfect or say the perfect things! When your intent genuinely embodies Competitive Kindness, you can speak with confidence even when your words aren't perfectly polished. Research on leader effectiveness shows that perceived intent accounts for 55 percent of communication impact, while actual words account for only 7 percent. People sense authentic Competitive Kindness, and it covers a multitude of communication imperfections.

2. Build Relationship Equity Through Competitive Kindness

When people know your heart embodies Competitive Kindness and trust your intentions, they extend grace to your words. The concept of "relationship equity" demonstrates that strong relationships create reserves of trust that enable more direct communication. Why does this matter? Studies have shown that leaders with high relationship equity can deliver difficult feedback with 70 percent better reception rates. If you need to deliver tough news to people, your relationship equity built through Competitive Kindness will literally soften the blow, so it is received. Real communication with intentionality will lead to winning.

3. Lead with Curiosity

Before jumping to conclusions, ask questions rooted in Competitive Kindness. "Help me understand what's happening here" or "Walk me through your thinking on this" removes defensiveness and invites collaboration. In research, this concept has been called "appreciative inquiry," which found that curiosity-based approaches to problem-solving generate three times as many creative solutions as deficit-focused questioning. If you're looking for innovation, try leading with competitively kind curiosity.

YOUR WORDS MATTER MORE THAN YOU KNOW

You don't need to be a perfect communicator to be an effective leader, but you do need to be intentional with your words through Competitive Kindness. Speaking with purpose isn't about walking on eggshells—it's about using your voice as an instrument of inspiration rather than a weapon of criticism.

Every day, you have countless opportunities to practice Competitive Kindness by helping people see their potential clearly. You can provide feedback that focuses on their growth rather than criticism that makes them shrink. You must capture hearts and minds while still driving exceptional results—that's Competitive Kindness in action.

In a world full of noise and negativity, your purposeful words rooted in Competitive Kindness can be a consistent source of clarity, encouragement, and growth. You're not choosing between being tough and being kind—you're choosing Competitive Kindness, which means being both. That's not just good leadership—it's smart business backed by decades of research demonstrating that positive leadership approaches consistently outperform punitive ones across every measurable outcome.

The question isn't whether your words have power. They do. The question is: will you use them as instruments of inspiration through Competitive Kindness, or as weapons of criticism that tear people down?

Remember, you may never know which casual conversation may become someone's turning point through Competitive Kindness—so make your words matter.

CHAPTER 15

PURSUE EXCELLENCE WITH COMPASSION

> People perform their best because they believe
> you're invested in their success. In a talent-driven world,
> compassionate excellence becomes a competitive advantage.
>
> *"How you win is just as important as whether you win."*
> Tony Dungy

HOMEBOY INDUSTRIES: PURSUING EXCELLENCE WITH COMPASSION

On the streets of East Los Angeles in the early nineties, where gang violence, poverty, and incarceration crushed hope, a radical idea was born—not through power, policy, or punishment, but through compassion. That idea became Homeboy Industries, now the largest gang rehabilitation and reentry program in the world.

Father Greg Boyle, a Jesuit priest affectionately known as "G," had seen over a hundred young people die in his congregation in a short period of time. Somebody had to do something to alter the community's fatal course. With that motivation, Homeboy Industries was born. It began with a revolutionary yet straightforward premise: "Nothing stops a bullet like a job." But it became much more than that. It became a movement of Competitive Kindness, grounded in the belief that everyone deserves a second chance—and that you can run a first-class organization while leading with compassion instead of ego. It also led to Father Boyle receiving the Presidential Medal of Freedom, an honor he never aspired to earn but was most deserving of.

At its core, Homeboy Industries is a model of excellence—not in traditional metrics like trophies or market share, but in transformational outcomes. Former gang members and previously incarcerated individuals enter the program broken, traumatized, and written off by society. Through a robust eighteen-month curriculum that offers therapy, education, tattoo removal, and employment in one of Homeboy's social enterprises (such as Homegirl Café or Homeboy Bakery), these individuals not only heal—they thrive.

One of those individuals is Mario.

When Mario first walked through the doors of Homeboy Industries, he carried the weight of multiple prison sentences, the scars of childhood trauma, and the belief that he was "beyond fixing." He was hardened, quiet, and angry. Years of gang life had taught him to hide vulnerability behind violence. But beneath that tough exterior was someone aching to be seen—not just as a criminal, but as a human being.

Father Boyle once said of Mario, "He'd never heard anyone say, 'I'm proud of you.' Not once in his life." And yet, slowly, surrounded by consistent love and relentless accountability, Mario began to change.

He enrolled in anger management, sat in therapy circles, and eventually took a job baking bread in the Homeboy Bakery. It wasn't just about learning a trade—it was about learning to trust, to show up, to let go of shame. He knew how to work a shift, lead a team, and believe in a future that wasn't dictated by his past.

Years later, Mario not only graduated from the program—he became a supervisor, a speaker, and a mentor to others still finding their way. He now stands in front of audiences and says, "I used to shoot people like you. Now I shake hands, and sometimes even hug you." The crowd usually laughs—but behind the humor is a profound truth: transformation is possible when people are treated with dignity instead of judgment.

Homeboy Industries doesn't lower standards to show compassion—it raises expectations through love, accountability, and belonging. Their rate of additional legal offenses is less than 30 percent, compared to a national average that often exceeds 65 percent. In business terms, that's market-beating performance. In human terms, that's a miraculous demonstration of elevating human dignity and potential.

Father Boyle teaches, "We imagine a circle of compassion, and then we imagine no one standing outside that circle." It's a philosophy that mirrors what Competitive Kindness demands—it's not choosing between results and relationships; instead, it's choosing results *AND* relationships.

To lead like Homeboy Industries, we elect to pursue greatness without leaving people behind. We can heal trauma while building something excellent. We will win with compassion.

UNDERSTANDING COMPASSION

Let's get something straight right off the bat: compassion isn't about being a pushover, and it's definitely not lowering your standards. In fact, genuine compassion often requires the courage to have difficult conversations and hold people accountable—because that's what helps them grow.

Compassion literally means "to suffer together," and among emotion researchers, it's defined as the feeling that arises when you are confronted with another's suffering and feel motivated to relieve that suffering. But here's what makes it powerful in leadership: compassion is an affective state that motivates a subsequent desire to help. It's not passive sympathy—it's active engagement. Compassion moves us to act.

In organizational settings, compassion becomes a collective noticing, feeling, and responding to suffering that promotes healing. Think about that for a moment. When your team is struggling with a problematic project, missing deadlines, or dealing with change, compassionate leadership means you notice the struggle, you feel it with them, and you actively respond in ways that promote healing and growth.

It isn't coddling people or making excuses for poor performance. It's recognizing that every person in your organization is fighting battles you know nothing about, carrying stress you can't see, and trying to do their best work while managing all the complexity of being human.

THE THREE COMPONENTS OF COMPASSION IN COMPETITIVE KINDNESS

Studies have found that compassion in the workplace operates through three distinct but interconnected components:

1. Noticing Suffering

Here is where most leaders fail before they even start. We're so focused on results, deadlines, metrics, and deliverables that we miss the subtle signs that our people are struggling. Maybe it's the usually collaborative team member who's gone quiet in meetings. Maybe it's the high performer whose work has suddenly become disengaged. Maybe it's the entire team that seems exhausted and frustrated.

Compassionate leaders develop peripheral vision for people. They're not just watching the numbers—they're watching for changes in energy, engagement, and emotional state.

2. Feeling with Others

It doesn't mean you become an emotional sponge, absorbing everyone else's stress and anxiety. That's a recipe for burnout. Instead, feeling with others means you allow yourself to be genuinely moved by what your team is experiencing. When they're frustrated, you sense and feel that frustration. When they're overwhelmed, you acknowledge it.

A growing body of evidence suggests compassion is a natural and automatic response that has ensured human survival. Your ability to connect emotionally with your team isn't a weakness—it's an evolutionary advantage that creates stronger, more resilient groups. As you strengthen this muscle, your evolutionary instincts of compassion will become stronger.

3. Responding to Help

Your response is where compassion transforms from feeling into leadership. It's not enough to notice and feel—you have to act. But here's the key: responding compassionately doesn't always mean making things easier. Sometimes the most compassionate response is to provide additional training, clearer expectations, or even performance improvement plans.

The question isn't "How can I remove all difficulty from this person's experience?" The question is "How can I respond in a way that helps them grow and advance toward their peak potential?" Your response to help teammates become the best version of themselves will develop into a superpower through compassionate leadership.

WHY COMPASSION WORKS
(THE SCIENCE BEHIND THE HEART)

Compassion plays a critical role in the workplace by promoting employee engagement, collaboration, productivity, retention, and organizational commitment. But let's dig into why this works, because the neuroscience is fascinating.

When people are led with compassion, the special sauce of psychological safety permeates throughout the organization with its incredible benefits. Google's *Project Aristotle* found that psychological safety—created primarily through compassionate leadership—was the number one factor distinguishing high-performing teams from average ones. What creates psychological safety? Leaders who combine high standards with genuine care for their people.

When people feel genuinely cared for, their brains literally work better under pressure. They take smarter risks, recover from failures faster, and—this is the big one—they don't burn out from being pushed hard. Physically and mentally healthy employees can focus better, make decisions more effectively, and sustain higher performance. People don't quit because you have high standards. They quit because you have high standards without really caring about them as human beings.

HOW TO BUILD COMPASSION INTO YOUR ORGANIZATION (THE IMPLEMENTATION BLUEPRINT)

Building a compassionate organization isn't about grand gestures or feel-good initiatives that fade after the first quarterly review. It's about creating systems, practices, and cultural norms that make compassion as natural as checking your email. Here's how to do it:

Start with Leadership Modeling

The good news is that becoming more compassionate is not only possible; it's actionable. Research shows that managers can grow in their own compassion by starting small, being thankful, being purposeful, finding common ground, and recognizing their power to influence others' experiences.

It means you go first. You're the one who admits when you're struggling. You're the one who asks for help when you need it. You're the one who shows vulnerability while maintaining strength. Your team is watching how you handle pressure, setbacks, and difficult conversations. They're learning what's acceptable, what's valued, and what's modeled.

One CEO I know starts every leadership team meeting by asking a simple question: "What's one thing you're struggling with right now, and how can we help?" It takes three minutes. It changes everything. People stop pretending that they have it all figured out and start problem-solving together.

Build Organizational Systems for Noticing

You can practice compassion at the workplace by continuously supporting and cheering others for their hard work and achievements, but it starts with simply noticing what's really happening with your people. Most organizations are brilliant at tracking quantitative productivity metrics and terrible at tracking qualitative human well-being metrics.

This part can be uncomfortable for many leaders that prefer metrics to emotions. Competitive Kindness in organizations can be systemized to build "noticing" into their regular rhythms. Here are seven examples of how to build compassion in noticing teammates:

REGULAR CHECK-INS BEYOND PERFORMANCE: Instead of just reviewing deliverables, leaders ask about workload, stress levels, and what support people need. This isn't therapy—it's strategic leadership. Overwhelmed people don't do their best work.

ENVIRONMENTAL AWARENESS: Create systems that enable leaders to regularly observe team dynamics, energy levels, and signs of struggle. This might be as simple as walking around and actually talking to people, or as sophisticated as employee pulse surveys that track well-being alongside performance. One Division I athletic director shared with me that he booked at least one hour per day to stop by people's offices throughout the organization to check in and see how they were doing.

PEER SUPPORT NETWORKS: Establish formal mentoring programs and informal buddy systems that specifically encourage people to support each other. When compassion is everyone's job, not just leadership's job, it becomes cultural.

Create Practical Response Mechanisms

The first step is to acknowledge and accept that pervasive suffering is actually happening in the workplace. Once you notice that people are struggling, you need systems to respond quickly and effectively. Do your teammates know where to go when they are struggling with anxiety? Do your people know with whom to talk if they are grieving the death of a colleague? This is where many well-intentioned leaders fall short—they care, but they don't act or know the next steps. Create simple systems that guide your team to know where to get answers.

FLEXIBLE SUPPORT OPTIONS: Sometimes, a compassionate response means adjusting deadlines. Sometimes it means providing additional resources or training. Sometimes it means having difficult conversations about performance. The key is having multiple tools in your toolkit, not just one.

EMPLOYEE ASSISTANCE PROGRAMS: Organizations need to prioritize mental health by implementing employee assistance programs, mental health awareness campaigns, and access to counseling services. But make sure these aren't just HR checkboxes—they need to be genuinely accessible and stigma-free. Otherwise, your efforts to lead with Competitive Kindness can quickly flip to Competitive Cruelty.

RECOVERY AND GROWTH PLANNING: When someone is struggling, work with them to create a clear and intentional plan for recovery and growth. This isn't about lowering standards—it's about creating a roadway back to excellence that acknowledges their humanity.

Implement Zero-Tolerance for Destructive Behavior

One way you can demonstrate organizational compassion is by adopting and formalizing a "zero-tolerance" approach to any abusive, underhanded, or discriminatory behavior on your team. Work with your HR team to structure and clearly communicate this policy.

This isn't about being the "nice" organization—it's about being the safe organization that is competitively kind. When people know they won't be attacked, undermined, or humiliated, they can focus their energy on doing great work instead of protecting themselves from colleagues.

PERSONAL COMPASSION SKILLS: THE INDIVIDUAL TOOLKIT

While organizational systems matter, compassion ultimately happens in individual interactions. Here are the specific skills that elevate Competitive Kindness through compassion:

The Art of Active Listening

You might wonder how to cultivate compassion in your professional life. Start by actively listening to your colleagues, acknowledging their feelings, and offering help when needed. But real listening goes deeper than just hearing words. Those we lead must feel validated, respected, valued, seen, and heard. If these feelings are not present, likely you need to listen more effectively. Keep practicing active listening a lifelong pursuit of excellence!

LISTEN FOR EMOTION, NOT JUST INFORMATION: When someone is explaining a problem, they're usually telling you two things: what happened and how they feel about what happened. Most leaders only respond to the first part. Compassionate leaders respond to both.

REFLECT BACK WHAT YOU HEAR: "It sounds like you're frustrated that your teammate is not doing his job and is pawning it off on you." This simple technique shows that you're not just waiting for your turn to talk—you're genuinely trying to understand their experience.

ASK QUESTIONS THAT SHOW YOU CARE: Instead of immediately jumping to solutions, ask questions that help you better understand their perspective. "What's been the hardest part about this for you?" "What would help most right now?"

Mastering Difficult Conversations with Compassion

Having difficult conversations is essential in Competitive Kindness where you do not abandon compassion—you apply it skillfully. When performance issues arise or when you need to deliver disappointing news, your approach means everything.

START WITH AFFIRMATION: Begin difficult conversations by acknowledging the person's value and your investment in their success. "I want to talk with you about this initiative because I believe your talents match up with this, and I want to see you succeed."

BE SPECIFIC ABOUT ISSUES, NOT PERSONAL CHARACTER: Focus on behaviors and outcomes, not personality traits. "You submitted the report two days late and missing the financial analysis section," rather than "You're irresponsible."

COLLABORATE ON SOLUTIONS: Instead of just identifying problems, work together to identify solutions. "What do you think would help you meet deadlines more consistently?" This approach maintains dignity while addressing performance.

A LIFE LESSON IN SOLUTIONS, NOT JUST SPOTTING PROBLEMS

Sometimes the most transformative leadership lessons come in unexpected moments. While serving a church mission in Romania and the Republic of Moldova, I coordinated assignments and service locations for 108 missionaries. It was complex work, and I took pride in my analytical skills for foreseeing future challenges and resolving them.

One day, I discovered what I believed was a significant administrative issue in how assignments were being handled. I was excited to bring this finding to the mission president, confident that he'd be impressed with my abilities and grateful for my diligence.

I walked into his office, presented the analysis of the problem, and waited for his praise and appreciation. Instead, he offered me something far more valuable—a lesson that would shape how I lead throughout my life.

He listened patiently, then responded with Competitive Kindness and unmistakable clarity: "Thank you for identifying this issue. But let me share something with you—almost anyone can spot problems.

True leaders don't just point out what's broken; they always come up with solutions."

In that moment, he wasn't just correcting my approach; he was teaching a young man a life lesson that was elevating my entire understanding of leadership responsibility. He could have thanked me and fixed the issue himself, or he could have dismissed my observation entirely. Instead, he saw an opportunity to teach a higher standard while affirming my potential.

"The next time you see something that needs fixing," he continued, "I want you to think through possible solutions before you bring it to me. Then make a recommendation based upon your excellent analysis. That's what leaders do—they solve, not just identify. So, knowing what you know about the situation, what would you recommend we do?"

This wasn't harsh criticism; it was compassionate correction. He maintained high expectations while helping me understand what Competitive Kindness looked like. That conversation fundamentally changed how I approach challenges—not as problems to delegate upward, but as opportunities to think strategically and offer real value.

That lesson in solution-oriented thinking has influenced every leadership role since, affecting thousands of people I've had the privilege to lead. It was Competitive Kindness in action—demanding excellence while developing potential, correcting behavior while building character.

George Jarvis, the mission president could have been grateful for my ability to identify the problem. Instead, he used that moment to teach me what it means to think like a leader. That's the power of pursuing excellence with compassion—it transforms not just performance, but people. For that, I am forever grateful to be introduced to compassionate and competitively kind leaders as a young man.

BUILDING PERSONAL EMOTIONAL RESILIENCE

Compassion in Competitive Kindness requires emotional strength, not emotional weakness. You need to be able to feel with your people without being overwhelmed by their emotions. It is critical for us to build personal emotional resilience, so that we can lead with Competitive Kindness. Here are some recommendations to build your emotional resilience:

- PRACTICE SELF-COMPASSION: Research shows that self-compassion is strongly related to team authenticity, psychological safety, and trust. You can't give what you don't have. Be kind to yourself when you make mistakes and model the emotional resilience you want to see in others. Speak positively to yourself in the mirror and throughout the day. If you aren't your biggest cheerleader, who will be?

- SET HEALTHY BOUNDARIES: Compassion doesn't mean taking responsibility for everyone else's emotions or problems. You can care deeply while maintaining clear boundaries about what you can and cannot control.

- REGULAR EMOTIONAL MAINTENANCE: Just like you maintain your physical health, you need to maintain your emotional health. This might mean regular exercise, meditation, therapy, religious worship, reading, listening to or playing music, artistic expression, or simply taking time to process the emotional demands of leadership.

CREATING MOMENTS OF CONNECTION

Some of the most potent examples of compassion demonstrated in Competitive Kindness leadership happen in small, everyday moments rather than grand gestures. Here are some suggestions on how to make these moments of connection happen:

- CELEBRATE PROGRESS, NOT JUST PERFECTION: Notice and acknowledge when people are making effort, learning from mistakes, or showing improvement. "I noticed how you handled that difficult client call—your patience made all the difference." This can be a text or brief conversation in the hallway. It's not about the magnitude—it's about the effort.

- REMEMBER PERSONAL DETAILS: Pay attention to what matters to your people outside of work. Ask about their loved ones, kids, their hobbies, and their goals. This isn't being nosy—it's being a good human.

- BE PRESENT IN CONVERSATIONS: When someone comes to talk with you, actually stop what you're doing. Put down the phone. Close the laptop. Give them your full attention with eye contact. Make sure your body language demonstrates that you are all-in on the conversation. In our multitasking world, presence is a gift.

COMPASSION MAKES THE DIFFERENCE IN THE TOUGH SITUATIONS

When both excellence and humanity are tested, compassion isn't just nice to have—it becomes essential in difficult situations:

- DURING CRISIS AND CHANGE: When organizations face layoffs, restructuring, or market upheaval, competitively kind leaders acknowledge the fear and uncertainty while maintaining clear direction. They don't sugarcoat reality, but they don't abandon people to face it alone.

- WHEN PEOPLE FAIL: Instead of punishment or removal, competitively kind leaders use the "Redemptive Loop"—What did you learn? Here's the consequence. Now, how do we move forward together? People who know they can recover from mistakes take smarter risks and innovate more.

- WITH HIGH PERFORMERS UNDER PRESSURE: Your top talent often carries the heaviest loads and faces the highest expectations. Having compassion means demonstrating effectively that they are valued by you and the organization. Competitively kind leaders will also watch for signs of burnout and proactively provide support before they break.

- IN DIVERSE AND INCLUSIVE ENVIRONMENTS: When people from different backgrounds, thinking preferences, life experiences, and perspectives work together, misunderstandings and conflicts are inevitable. Compassion creates psychological safety, enabling honest dialogue and mutual learning. What some may consider a tough environment becomes a beautiful blend of organizational success and empowering individual worth.

As research shows, when individuals feel safe contributing without fear of ridicule or rejection, they are more likely to share their unique insights, leading to enhanced collaboration and better problem-solving outcomes.

THE BOTTOM LINE: PUSH, BUT DON'T BREAK

Compassion does not lower standards to become everyone's best friend. We must create environments where people give their best, not because they're afraid of you, but because they believe in the vision and that you're invested in their success. Your compassion leads to their intrinsic motivation.

Here's what pursuing excellence with compassion looks like in practice:

- Set standards that stretch people without snapping them
- Give feedback that sharpens performance, acknowledges their potential, and builds their confidence
- Offer grace that restores people without removing responsibility

Your team will forget your presentations, your strategic initiatives, and most of your brilliant insights. But they'll never forget how you made them feel while they were growing.

That's not just good leadership—it's Competitive Kindness disguised as human decency. And in a world where talent is the ultimate differentiator, it might just be the edge that separates you from everyone else.

The question isn't whether you should lead with Competitive Kindness that pursues excellence with compassion. The question we should ask ourselves is "Why wouldn't you?"

CHAPTER 16

WHAT TO DO WHEN BEING KIND FEELS IMPOSSIBLE OR UNNATURAL

When your patience is low, your emotions are high,
and others are testing your limits, there is a navigation system
to help you lead with Competitive Kindness.

*"Success is about leaving a legacy of generosity and kindness
rather than a trail of destruction."*
Crystal Eisinger

Competitive Kindness isn't all sunshine and rainbows. Let's have some real talk about the brutal days—you know, the days when being kind feels like the hardest thing in the world.

You may be dealing with a team member who keeps making the same mistakes despite your patience and competitively kind correction. Maybe you're facing a competitor who's playing dirty, which has brought about real danger or pain to you or a teammate. Maybe you're under crushing pressure from fear-based leadership above you while trying to shield your team from the negativity. Maybe you're watching cruelty win while kindness is starting to feel like a losing strategy.

I get it. I've been there. We all have.

And if you're reading this and wondering how to stay kind when everything in you is wanting to snap, when being gracious feels like giving up or allowing people to walk all over you, when choosing compassion feels like choosing to lose—this is for you.

Because the moments when Competitive Kindness feels impossible are precisely the moments when it matters most. More importantly, there are real, practical ways to choose grace, when kindness might feel unnatural for you or even when your heart is heavy and your patience is gone.

THE R FACTOR: YOUR SECRET WEAPON WHEN COMPETITIVE KINDNESS FEELS IMPOSSIBLE

Before we dive deeper, I want to introduce you to the most powerful tool you have for leading with kindness under challenging moments: your Response.

Years ago, I was an emerging executive in intercollegiate athletics struggling with many of the challenges outlined a few moments ago. I was attending a national conference for athletics administrators, and I stumbled upon a session that would alter my daily mindset for the rest of my life. The founder and CEO of Focus 3, Tim Kight, was talking about the R-Factor. At first, I was dismissive and skeptical, assuming this was just another one of those motivational speakers like Chris Farley hilariously imitated on Saturday Night Live in the nineties. After dozens of championship head football coaches shared testimonials about the championship impact of this formula, I decided it was time I should humble myself enough to be taught. This is the simple but profound formula:

$$E + R = O$$

Event + Response = Outcome

The Events that happen to you—the difficult team members, the unfair criticism, the crushing pressure—those are largely outside your control. But your Response? That's 100 percent on you. And your Response is more important in determining your Outcome.

This is what Kight calls the R Factor: "Your Response is your power."

When Competitive Kindness feels impossible, you're not powerless. You still have your R Factor. You still get to choose how you respond. And that choice—that's where Competitive Kindness lives.

THE NORTH STAR MEETS ITS NAVIGATION SYSTEM

Competitive Kindness is fundamentally an ethos—a way of being that integrates strength with deliberate thoughtfulness, results with relationships, and winning with dignity. It's rooted in foundational characteristics that are developed intrinsically, which manifest externally to elevate everyone involved to become the best version of ourselves.

The R Factor, by contrast, is an operational framework—a systematic approach to decision-making under pressure. Here's what I've discovered: the R Factor becomes exponentially more powerful when it's rooted in Competitive Kindness. And Competitive Kindness becomes infinitely more practical when it's operationalized through the R Factor framework.

Think of it this way: leading with Competitive Kindness is your north star—your fundamental commitment to leading to maximize organizational and individual human potential with both strength and grace. The R Factor is your navigation system—the practical tool that helps you move toward that north star even when the weather gets rough and visibility is poor.

THE ROADMAP OF R FACTOR DISCIPLINES

Kight teaches six specific R Factor disciplines that empower you to respond with intention, purpose, and skill—even when being competitively kind feels impossible. These six disciplines become your roadmap for Competitive Kindness under pressure:

- R1: PRESS PAUSE—Before reacting, ask "What does this situation require of me?"
- R2: GET YOUR MIND RIGHT—Manage what you focus on and how you talk to yourself
- R3: STEP UP—Take responsibility and respond above the line
- R4: Adjust and Adapt—Stay flexible and responsive to challenging circumstances
- R5: MAKE A DIFFERENCE—Remember your response becomes an event for others
- R6: BUILD SKILL—Continuously develop your ability to choose kindness under pressure

Every challenging moment or interaction becomes an opportunity to ask: "What response will create the Outcome I want? What response aligns with the leader I'm committed to being? What response aligns with the kind of person I am committed to being?" The six R Factor disciplines give you the framework to answer those questions with Competitive Kindness.

THE REALITY CHECK:
WHY COMPETITIVE KINDNESS FEELS SO DIFFICULT

Let's acknowledge what few want to admit—leading with Competitive Kindness can be seriously exhausting. Choosing Competitive Cruelty is easier in the moment. It's faster to be harsh. It's more immediately satisfying to unleash the fury when someone has disappointed you.

Competitive Kindness requires you to:

- Pause when human nature screams at you to react emotionally
- Seek understanding when you want to render cruel judgment
- Extend grace while maintaining accountability to the standard of excellence
- Believe in people's potential when they've given you evidence to the contrary

- Remain vulnerable when you want to build protective walls
- Choose long-term relationship building over short-term emotional satisfaction

And sometimes, after you've chosen kindness over and over, you look around and wonder if you're the only one playing by these rules. You wonder if your gentleness is being mistaken for weakness. You wonder if you're being taken advantage of.

These feelings are normal. They're also where the real work begins.

Here's the truth: the Event (someone disappointing you, attacking you, or taking advantage of your kindness) is going to happen. You can't control that. But you can absolutely control your Response. And when you consistently respond with Competitive Kindness, the Outcomes speak for themselves. You will build stronger teams, deeper trust, better performance, and sustainable success.

FIVE COMMITMENTS OF A COMPETITIVE KINDNESS LEADER

When Kindness feels impossible, recommit to these disciplines that sharpen your R Factor through the six disciplines:

1. Lead with Courageous Clarity (R1 & R3: Pause and Step Up)

Kindness doesn't mean avoiding hard truths. It means pausing to understand what the situation requires, then stepping up to deliver truth with care. Your Response should always include clarity delivered with love.

"Clarity is kind. Confusion is not." – Brené Brown

2. **Practice Micro-Consistency (R2 & R6: Mental Management and Skill Building)**

People remember how you show up in the small moments. Your Response to a dropped pass, a missed deadline, a tough email—these build your reputation for Competitive Kindness. Get your mind right for each interaction and build skill through consistent practice. Small Responses equal big Outcomes.

3. **Choose Presence Over Posture (R1 & R5: Pause and Make a Difference)**

Put the phone down. Look people in the eye. Respond thoughtfully. Press pause on your agenda and focus on what this person needs. Your Response of full attention becomes a positive Event in their day, especially when it's least convenient.

4. **Stand Firm in Grace (R3 & R4: Step Up and Adapt)**

Holding someone accountable IS a kind Response—when it's done with grace. Step up to take responsibility for clear expectations, then adapt your approach to reinforce standards while protecting both dignity and direction.

5. **Model Recovery, Not Perfection (R1, R2, & R6: Pause, Reset, and Grow)**

When your Response falls short—and it will sometimes—press pause, get your mind right, and build skill from the experience. Apologize quickly. Repair the moment. That humble Response models Competitive Kindness at a whole new level.

WHEN YOUR PATIENCE IS GONE: THE EMERGENCY KINDNESS TOOLKIT

When you're at your breaking point and someone needs your leadership, here's your emergency playbook—all designed around owning your R Factor:

The Five-Second Rule (R1: Press Pause in Action)

Before you speak, count to five. Not in your head—literally count. "One Mississippi, two Mississippi..." It sounds silly, but it works. Those five seconds create space between the Event and your Response. Space is where wisdom can enter.

This is R1: Press Pause in action. In those five seconds, ask yourself: "What does this situation require of me?" It helps you avoid doing something foolish or harmful while focusing you on acting with purpose to accomplish your goals.

The E+R=O Reset (R2: Get Your Mind Right)

When something frustrating happens, immediately think:

- Event: What just occurred? (State it factually, without emotion)
- Response: What response will create the Outcome I want?
- Outcome: What am I trying to achieve here?

This mental reset embodies R2: Get Your Mind Right. You're managing what you focus on (the facts, not your emotional story) and how you talk to yourself (solution-focused, not victim-focused). This reset takes ten seconds and transforms your brain from reactive to responsive.

Assume Positive Intent (R2: Get Your Mind Right in Practice)

When someone disappoints you, you must get your mind right because:

- Your brain floods with cortisol and immediately writes a story about why: "They don't care. They're lazy. They're trying to make me look bad."
- Instead, force yourself to assume positive intent first. Ask yourself: "What if they're struggling? What if they're overwhelmed? What if they're dealing with something I don't know about?"

This is R2: Get Your Mind Right in action—you're taking ownership of the voice in your mind and choosing what to focus on. It doesn't mean lowering your standards. It means selecting a Response that starts with curiosity rather than judgment. The Event is the same: someone didn't meet expectations. But your Response lens determines whether the Outcome is defensive and destructive or constructive and growth oriented.

The Reporter's Technique (R3: Step Up with Facts)

When you're angry, you speak like a prosecutor. When you're disappointed, you talk like a judge. When you're frustrated, you speak like a victim. Instead, speak like a reporter. State facts without editorializing:

- "The project was due yesterday, and it wasn't delivered."
- "We discussed these mistakes in our one-on-one last Friday."
- The client called to express their concern."

This embodies R3: Step Up—you're taking responsibility to understand the situation clearly and respond above the line. Facts without emotional overlay give you a foundation for kind but clear communication. You're choosing a Response that focuses on what happened (the Event) rather than your emotional reaction to it.

The Redirect Method (R4: Adjust and Adapt Your Language)

When you feel Competitive Cruelty rising, redirect it immediately:

- Instead of "You always…" try "I've noticed…"
- Instead of "You never…" try "I need…"
- Instead of "You're…" try "This situation is…"

This demonstrates R4: Adjust and Adapt—you're being flexible and responsive to challenging circumstances by adapting your communication approach. This is your R Factor in action—taking a frustrating Event and choosing a Response that opens doors rather than closing them. The ability to adjust your language in real-time is a critical skill for Competitive Kindness.

WHEN YOU'RE UNDER ATTACK: THE R FACTOR UNDER PRESSURE

The hardest time to be kind is when someone is being unkind to you. When you're being criticized unfairly, blamed for things beyond your control, lied about, or treated with disrespect, every instinct tells you to fight fire with fire.

But remember: their attack is the Event but your Response is your power. Here's how to stay kind without becoming a doormat:

The R Factor Mindset Shift (R5: Make a Difference)

The moment someone attacks you, remind yourself:

- "This is not about me. This is about them. My Response is about me."

This embodies R5: Make a Difference—remembering that your Response becomes an Event for others. Their behavior is the Event. It reveals something about their stress, fear, pain, or character. Your Response reveals something about you and becomes the Event that shapes their following response. You have the power to break negative cycles through your Response choices.

Acknowledge the Emotion, Address the Issue

- "I can see you're frustrated, and I want to understand what's driving that. Help me see this from your perspective."
- It validates their feelings without accepting inappropriate behavior. It keeps you in control of the conversation while showing you're willing to listen. You're choosing a Response that de-escalates rather than escalates.

Use the Aikido Principle (Redirecting Energy)

In Japanese martial arts, Aikido teaches you to redirect an opponent's energy rather than meet it head-on. From the Competitive Kindness lens, this means:

- "You're right to be concerned about this. Let's figure out how to fix it."
- "I understand why this is upsetting. What would success look like for you?"
- "That's a fair point. How do you think we should move forward?"

You're not agreeing with their approach, but you're redirecting their energy toward solutions. The Event is their attack. Your Response focuses on collaboration and problem-solving.

Set Boundaries with Grace (Response with Strength)

At times, kindness means saying no. Sometimes it means stopping a conversation that's become unproductive. You can do this gracefully:

- "I want to give this the attention it deserves. Let's schedule time to discuss this when we have both adequately prepared meaningful solutions."
- "I can see we're both frustrated. Let's take a break and revisit this when we can be more productive."
- "I'm committed to working through this with you, but I need us to keep our conversation respectful."

This is Competitive Kindness at its finest—you're being kind and strong. This approach is both empowering and enlightening. You're controlling your Response to create an Outcome that serves everyone.

WHEN YOUR TEAM DISAPPOINTS YOU: LEADING THROUGH LETDOWN

One of the most complex parts of leadership is watching people you've invested in make choices that disappoint you. When you've believed in someone and they've let you down. When you've given opportunities and they've wasted them. When you've extended trust and they've broken it.

The Event hurts. But your Response as a leader will determine whether this becomes a moment of destruction or development. Let Competitive Kindness be your north star in your Response.

The E+R=O Leadership Framework

Event: Someone you trusted let you down.

Response:

- Option A: React with anger, write them off, make them feel small
- Option B: Respond with disappointed clarity, focus on learning and growth.

Outcomes:

- Option A: Damaged relationship, defensive employee, missed learning opportunity
- Option B: Preserved relationship, accountable employee, stronger future performance

Separate the Person from the Performance

Your team member isn't a failure. They failed at something. That's a crucial distinction that keeps the door open for growth and redemption.

- Say: "This didn't work out the way we hoped. Let's figure out what went wrong and how to do better next time."
- Not: "You really dropped the ball on this one."

Remember that your Response shapes their identity and their future performance.

Focus on the Future, Not the Past (The Forward-Looking Response)

Dwelling on what went wrong feels satisfying, but it isn't helpful. Pointing the finger of blame, complaining about what went wrong, or defending mistakes of the past will not help performance in the future. Competitively kind leaders spend 20 percent of their time understanding what happened and 80 percent focused on what comes next.

- "I'm disappointed in how this turned out. Now, what do we need to do differently as we advance?"

The Event already happened. Your Response determines whether you stay stuck in the past or move toward a better future.

Give Them the Gift of Clarity (Response with Purpose)

Sometimes the kindest thing you can do is be crystal clear about what needs to change. Vague feedback helps no one. Specific, actionable guidance shows you care enough to help them succeed.

- "Here's exactly what I need to see differently..." is more helpful than "You need to step up your game."

Your Response should always serve the Outcome of their growth and success.

THE HARDEST MOMENTS: R FACTOR IN ACTION

Every leader will face incredibly difficult decisions. It's even tougher when these decisions are Events that are the direct result of other people's poor Response. Here are ways to respond with Competitive Kindness to some of the toughest moments:

When You Have to Let Someone Go

Event: Someone's performance requires termination

Kind Response: Focus on dignity, clarity, and support

- Be clear about the decision and the reasons for the separation
- Acknowledge their contributions and strengths
- Offer support for their transition
- Protect their dignity throughout the process

When You're Getting Blamed for Others' Mistakes

Event: You're being blamed unfairly

Strong Response: Stay factual and avoid defensive reactions

- Stay calm and stick to facts
- Resist the urge to throw others under the bus
- Take responsibility for your part without accepting blame for things beyond your control
- Address the situation privately with the individuals involved

When Your Kindness is Being Exploited

Event: Someone is taking advantage of your kindness

Boundary Response: Be kind but clear about limits

- Set clear boundaries about what's acceptable
- Be kind but not naïve
- Correct the behavior directly but respectfully
- Don't let one person's poor choices change your approach to everyone else

BUILDING YOUR R FACTOR MUSCLE: THE SIX DISCIPLINES IN DAILY PRACTICE

Leading with Competitive Kindness requires building your Response muscle using the six R Factor disciplines. Here are daily practices that will strengthen your ability to choose grace under pressure:

R1: Press Pause — The Daily Pause Practice

Throughout the day, practice making use of the pause between Event and Response. Start with minor annoyances—the slow elevator, traffic jams, the long line, the dropped call. Ask yourself: "What does this situation require of me?" Use these moments to build your muscle for bigger challenges.

R2: Get Your Mind Right – The Daily Mental Management

Every morning, set your mental focus: "What will I focus on today? How will I talk to myself when things get difficult?" During challenging moments, actively manage your internal dialogue. Replace "This is terrible" with "This is challenging, and I can handle it."

R3: Step Up – The Daily Responsibility Check

Before each interaction, remind yourself: "I am responsible for my Response. I will respond above the line." Take ownership of the experience you create for others through your Responses.

R4: Adjust and Adapt – The Daily Flexibility Practice

When your initial approach isn't working, quickly adjust. Practice saying: "That approach isn't working. Let me try a different way." Build your skill in real-time adaptation.

R5: Make a Difference – The Daily Impact Awareness

Remember that your Response becomes an Event for others. Ask yourself: "How do I want people to feel after interacting with me? What kind of Event do I want to be in their day?"

R6: Build Skill – The Daily Growth Commitment

Commit to getting 1 percent better at Competitive Kindness every day. Read about it, practice it, get feedback on it. Embrace the discomfort of growth. If it doesn't challenge you, it won't change you.

Regularly, review your calendar through the six R Factor disciplines:

- R1: When did I pause effectively? When did I react too quickly?
- R2: How well did I manage my focus and self-talk?
- R3: Where did I step up? Where did I fall short in taking responsibility?
- R4: How flexible was I when my initial approach didn't work?
- R5: What kind of Event was I for others today?
- R6: How did I build my Competitive Kindness skills today?

Using the discipline will build your awareness of the pattern and strengthen your ability to choose better Responses in real time.

The Response Rehearsal (R6: Build Skill Intentionally)

Before difficult conversations or stressful situations, mentally rehearse your desired Response using all six R Factor disciplines:

- R1: How will I pause and assess what the situation requires?
- R2: What will I focus on and how will I talk to myself?
- R3: How will I step up and take responsibility?
- R4: How will I stay flexible if my initial approach doesn't work?
- R5: What kind of positive Event do I want to be for this person?
- R6: How can I use this interaction to build my Competitive Kindness skills?

Remember, the foundation of Competitive Kindness requires unwavering integrity, authenticity, and humility. No Event should ever change that. Which is why "Your Response is your power," and Competitive Kindness is your north star. When you allow the six R Factor disciplines to guide your approach to choice, you are working to become the best version of yourself.

WHEN THE WORLD FEELS CRUEL: PROTECTING YOUR HEART WHILE STAYING STRONG

Leading with kindness in an unkind world can feel like you're swimming upstream. You'll face people who mistake your kindness for weakness, competitors who see your integrity as a liability, and environments that reward cruelty over compassion. Remember: their cruelty is the Event. Your unyielding kindness is your Response. And your Response is building an Outcome that's bigger than any single interaction. Take time to intentionally build your resilience by:

Finding Your Competitive Kindness Community

You aren't the only kind person in your world. Seek out other leaders who share your values and understand the R Factor. Join communities, attend conferences where kindness is celebrated, not just tolerated.

Inject Your Life With Inspiration

Read books, listen to podcasts, study scripture, or other inspirations that feed the foundation and pillars of Competitive Kindness in your heart. When you make this a daily practice, your resilience will grow.

CELEBRATE YOUR R FACTOR WINS

Notice when your Response created a positive Outcome. You resolved the conflict through your grace—the team member grew because of your patience. The culture shifted because of your consistency. Keep a journal or notes on your phone to record these moments. On hard days, it will remind you that your R Factor is making a difference.

Remember: You're Building Something Bigger!

Every time you choose Competitive Kindness as a Response when it would be easier to select cruelty, you're not just leading—you're modeling. You're proving that another way is possible. You're showing everyone around you that strength and gentleness can coexist.

LEADERSHIP SELF-CHECK: AM I USING MY R FACTOR FOR COMPETITIVE KINDNESS?

In your efforts to build your Response muscle to lead with Competitive Kindness, here are some questions that you can ask yourself to see where you stand:

- R1: PRESS PAUSE—Do I pause to ask "What does this situation require of me?" before responding?

- R2: GET YOUR MIND RIGHT—Am I managing what I focus on and how I talk to myself under pressure?
- R3: STEP UP—Do I take responsibility and respond above the line consistently?
- R4: ADJUST AND ADAPT—Am I flexible when my initial approach isn't working?
- R5: MAKE A DIFFERENCE—Do people leave my presence feeling smaller or stronger?
- R6: BUILD SKILL—Am I intentionally building my foundation and pillars of Competitive Kindness daily?

Some additional questions you can ask as you advance in your development of Competitive Kindness Response muscles:

- Would my staff say my Responses demonstrate both empathy and accountability?
- Are my daily Responses building the culture I want to create?

If you're asking those questions honestly and working through the six R Factor disciplines, you're already becoming a leader with Competitive Kindness that others want to follow.

YOUR RESPONSE IS YOUR POWER— ESPECIALLY WHEN IT'S HARD

The moments when Competitive Kindness feels impossible are the moments when your R Factor matters most. When you're exhausted, frustrated, disappointed, or under attack—that's when choosing Competitive Kindness for your Response becomes an act of courage.

You don't have to be perfect. You don't have to have unlimited patience. You don't have to be perpetually understanding. You have to keep choosing kind Responses, one difficult moment at a time.

Because the world has enough harsh leaders. It has enough disrespect and mudslinging. It has enough people who lead through fear and intimidation. It has enough examples of what happens when Events trigger cruel Responses.

It needs more leaders like you—people who understand that true strength lies in choosing compassionate Responses even when Events are costly, gracious Responses even when Events are complex, and loving Responses even when Events feel undeserving. Your Response matters. Especially when it's difficult. Especially when it feels impossible. Especially when no one else is watching. Especially when you're exhausted.

It's exactly when your R Factor matters most.

Remember the wisdom that: "Your Response is your power." The Event may break your heart, but your Response reveals your character. And when you consistently choose Competitive Kindness in your Responses, you create Outcomes that change everything for everyone around you.

Being kind doesn't mean being weak. It means being strong enough in your values that you can afford gentle Responses. So confident in your leadership that you don't need to tear others down to build yourself up. So secure in your purpose that you can lead with your heart, even when Events are breaking it.

The world needs more leaders who understand this. The world needs more leaders who know their Response is their power.

The world needs more competitively kind leaders like you.

CHAPTER 17

YOUR CHOICE AGAINST THE HEADWINDS

Here's the moment. You've heard the case for Competitive Kindness, but you have a choice to make. What will it be?

"Kindness is the essence of greatness and the fundamental characteristic of the most noble men and women I have known."
Joseph Wirthlin

THE FOUR LAWS THAT GOVERN YOUR CHOICE

Every aircraft that has ever taken flight—from the Wright brothers' first twelve-second journey to today's transcontinental jets—operates under four fundamental laws of physics: Weight, Drag, Thrust, and Lift. These same forces that determine whether a plane soars or crashes also govern how we lead people and shape organizational culture. Understanding these laws gives us a framework for choosing between Competitive Kindness and Competitive Cruelty in every leadership moment.

WEIGHT: WHAT PULLS US DOWN

In aviation, weight is the downward force created by gravity acting on the aircraft's mass. Too much weight, and the plane cannot lift off the ground. In leadership, weight represents the burdens we carry and impose on others—fear, insecurity, past failures, and toxic patterns. Leaders operating under excessive emotional weight create gravity wells that pull entire teams toward the ground.

Competitive Cruelty adds weight through micromanagement born of distrust, criticism rooted in insecurity, and the accumulated mass of unresolved leadership wounds. These leaders become black holes, making everyone around them feel heavier.

Competitive Kindness reduces weight by creating psychological safety, offering genuine encouragement, and helping others release the unnecessary burdens they carry. Kind leaders become sources of light that make it easier for others to rise.

DRAG: WHAT RESISTS FORWARD MOTION

In aviation, Drag is the force that opposes thrust, created by air resistance and anything that disrupts smooth airflow around the aircraft. Simply put, drag will slow you down as you fly. In leadership, drag manifests as resistance to progress—both the external drag from difficult people and circumstances, and the internal drag from our own reluctance to change and grow.

Competitive Cruelty creates drag through constant criticism, decisions being made for self-preservation, resistance to new ideas, and the turbulence of interpersonal conflict. Cruel leaders generate organizational headwinds that make forward progress exhausting for everyone. Competitive Kindness minimizes drag by addressing conflicts through correction, embracing change with grace, and creating smooth relational dynamics. Competitively kind leaders reduce friction and drive their teams to move forward with less resistance.

THRUST: WHAT PROPELS US FORWARD

In aviation, Thrust is the forward force generated by engines or propellers that moves the aircraft forward through the air. In leadership, thrust comes from clarity of purpose, strength of conviction, and the disciplined action that follows clear thinking. It's the forward momentum that drives achievement and progress.

Competitive Cruelty generates false thrust through fear-based motivation, unsustainable pressure, and short-term thinking. It creates movement, but it's ultimately unsustainable, physically and emotionally damaging, and often misdirected. Whereas Competitive Kindness creates sustainable *momentum* through shared vision, intrinsic motivation, and long-term relationship-building. Competitively kind leaders generate momentum that grows stronger over time rather than burning out.

LIFT: WHAT HELPS US SOAR

In aviation, Lift is the upward force that counteracts weight, created when air moves faster over the top of the wing than underneath it. This mysterious force allows objects heavier than air to rise and soar. In leadership, lift is the most potent and transformative force—the ability to elevate others and create environments where people and organizations rise above their circumstances.

Competitive Cruelty destroys life by creating environments where people feel diminished, criticized, and small. Cruel leaders may achieve temporary results through force, but they cannot create sustainable elevation. However, Competitive Kindness generates extraordinary lift by believing in others' potential, celebrating their contributions, inspiring them to become their best selves, and creating conditions where everyone can rise. Kind leaders don't just achieve results—they help others discover they can fly.

FLYING INTO THE HEADWINDS

Winning is hard. Producing results in your field of competition is expected. This environment where we lead creates heavy winds of opposition—which in aviation is called a headwind. The most skilled pilots don't avoid headwinds—they use them strategically. Taking off into a headwind actually creates more lift, allowing for shorter runway distances and better control. The resistance that seems like an obstacle becomes a winning edge. Herein lies the power of Competitive Kindness: it transforms opposition into opportunity. When you choose kindness in the face of cruelty, criticism, or conflict, you're not just taking the moral high ground—you're gaining altitude that your competitors cannot reach.

Leaders who master Competitive Kindness learn to convert:

- Criticism into clarity about their values
- Conflict into opportunities for deeper connection
- Setbacks into setups for stronger comebacks
- Resistance is the very force that lifts them higher

YOUR CHOICE IN EVERY MOMENT

Every interaction you have as a leader involves all four forces. You can choose to add weight or lift people up. You can generate sustainable thrust or drag people into burn out. Most importantly, you can choose to create lift that helps others soar while driving your team forward through Competitive Kindness.

The leaders who master Competitive Kindness understand something profound: the same forces that can keep you grounded are the very forces that can help you soar. The difference isn't in avoiding the headwinds—it's in how you choose to respond to them.

THE COMPETITIVE KINDNESS ADVANTAGE

Here's what the research tells us about leaders who consistently choose
Competitive Kindness:

- Their teams show 31 percent higher productivity
- Their organizations experience 40 percent lower turnover
- They achieve 37 percent better sales performance
- Their employees are three-times more likely to stay engaged

But beyond the metrics lies a more profound truth: Competitive Kindness
doesn't just produce better results—it cultivates the human spirit to soar
to greater heights. Competitively kind leaders don't just build successful
organizations; they build human beings who become the best version of
themselves, and they go on to lift others to do the same.

YOUR FLIGHT PLAN FORWARD

As you close this book and return to the cockpit of your leadership
responsibilities, remember that you face the same four forces that govern
every flight. The weight of responsibility and past experiences will always
be there. The drag of difficult circumstances and challenging people is
inevitable. But you have control over your thrust—your sense of purpose
and forward momentum. And most importantly, you can choose to
generate lift through Competitive Kindness.

THE R FACTOR: YOUR PRE-FLIGHT CHECK

Before every flight, pilots complete a rigorous pre-flight check to ensure
safe passage. As a leader, you need your own pre-flight protocol. Use the
R Factor as your daily checkpoint for Competitive Kindness:

- RECOGNIZE the moment when you feel the pull toward Competitive
  Cruelty—the critical comment on your tongue, the impulse to
  withhold credit, the temptation to respond to pressure with pressure.

- REFLECT on what this moment demands of you as a leader. What would the leader you aspire to be do right now? What would create lift instead of weight?
- RESPOND with intentional Competitive Kindness—not because it's easy, but because it's the choice that will elevate everyone around you and set you apart from leaders who default to Competitive Cruelty under pressure.

This is your competitive advantage: while others react, you respond. While others create turbulence, you generate lift. While others fight the headwinds, you use them to soar higher. The question isn't whether or not you'll face headwinds—you will. The question is whether or not you'll leverage the R Factor to transform them into the very force that lifts you above your competition.

Every day, you choose your altitude. In every interaction, you decide whether to create turbulence or smooth air. Every challenge, you determine whether to fight the headwinds or use them to rise higher.

The runway is clear. Your destination is set. The choice is yours to lead with Competitive Kindness—especially when it's hardest.

Push the throttle forward and prepare for liftoff. The world needs Competitive Kindness. And your team needs you.

Dare to lead differently! Dare to be kind!

ACKNOWLEDGMENTS

This book exists because of the people who inspired me by the way they bring humanity and decency while striving to be their best as leaders. The essence of Competitive Kindness.

I am grateful for Team Clark (my family). You are the foundation of everything. Emily, your guidance and unwavering daily commitment to kindness became the lighthouse of this book. You don't just talk about these principles; you live them, especially when it's hardest. Annie, Kate, and McCoy, you are my inspiration to win and to win the right way every single day. Watching you navigate the challenges of moving around the country, the setbacks, and the triumphs has taught me as much as I could ever teach you. You show me why it matters how we compete.

Thank you to my parents and sisters—you each filled our home with love and spunk while we lifted each other to become the best version of ourselves. A special shout out to Jaime for believing in the importance of starting the Competitive Kindness movement through this book.

My appreciation to the mentors, coaches, and leaders that I've been privileged to work alongside—in boardrooms, on fields and courts of play, and in church service alike—thank you for modeling Competitive Kindness. You have shown me that strength and compassion aren't opposing forces but complementary ones. Your wisdom appears throughout these pages, even if your names don't.

Above all, I acknowledge the greatest source of strength in my life, Jesus Christ. He is the ultimate exemplar of Competitive Kindness. His life demonstrated that we can be both driven and loving, ambitious and humble, both victorious and gracious. He showed us that the highest form of winning is lifting others as we ascend to the greatest heights imaginable.

This book is my attempt to honor what you have all taught me. Any wisdom found here is a reflection of your influence. Any shortcomings are entirely my own.

WORKS CITED

CHAPTER 3: COMPETITIVE KINDNESS IS MORE THAN BEING NICE

1. Boyatzis, R. E., Smith, M. L., & Blaize, N. (2006). Developing sustainable leaders through coaching and compassion. *Academy of Management Learning & Education,* 5(1), 8–24.

2. Cameron, K. S., et al. (2004). Positive organizational scholarship: Foundations of a new discipline. *Berrett-Koehler.*

3. Duckworth, A. (2016). Grit: *The Power of Passion and Perseverance.* Scribner.

4. Edmondson, A. (1999). Psychological safety and learning behavior in work teams. *Administrative Science Quarterly,* 44(2), 350–383.

5. Kapitulik, E., & Hernandez, J. (2019). *The Program: Lessons from Elite Military Units for Creating and Sustaining High Performance Leaders and Teams.*

6. Walton, G. M., & Cohen, G. L. (2007). A brief social-belonging intervention improves academic and health outcomes of minority students. *Science,* 331(6023), 1447–1451.

7. Lilius, J. M., et al. (2008). The contours and consequences of compassion at work. *Journal of Organizational Behavior,* 29(2), 193–218.

8. Kahn, W. A. (1990). Psychological conditions of personal engagement and disengagement at work. *Academy of Management Journal,* 33(4), 692–724

CHAPTER 4: THE HIDDEN PRICE OF COMPETITIVE CRUELTY

9. American Institute of Stress. (2023). *Workplace stress statistics.* https://www.stress.org/workplace-stress

10. Baumeister, R. F., & Vohs, K. D. (2007). Self-regulation, ego depletion, and motivation. *Social and Personality Psychology Compass,* 1(1), 115–128. https://doi.org/10.1111/j.1751-9004.2007.00001.x

11. Einarsen, S., Aasland, M. S., & Skogstad, A. (2007). Destructive leadership behaviour: A definition and conceptual model. *The Leadership Quarterly,* 18(3), 207–216. https://doi.org/10.1016/j.leaqua.2007.03.002Gallup. (2023). State of the global workplace: 2023 report. https://www.gallup.com/workplace

12. Glomb, T. M., Duffy, M. K., Bono, J. E., & Yang, T. (2011). Mindfulness at work. *Research in Personnel and Human Resources Management,* 30, 115–157. https://doi.org/10.1108/S0742-7301(2011)0000030006

13. Goleman, D., Boyatzis, R., & McKee, A. (2013). *Primal leadership: Unleashing the power of emotional intelligence*. Harvard Business Review Press.

14. Harvard Human Flourishing Program. (2021). *Virtues and human flourishing research*. https://hfh.fas.harvard.edu

15. Kabat-Zinn, J. (2015). *Mindfulness for beginners: Reclaiming the present moment—and your life*. Sounds True.

16. Kouchaki, M., & Smith, I. H. (2014). The morning morality effect: The influence of time of day on unethical behavior. *Psychological Science*, 25(1), 95–102. https://doi.org/10.1177/0956797613496435

17. Lilius, J. M., Worline, M. C., Maitlis, S., Kanov, J., Dutton, J. E., & Frost, P. J. (2008). The contours and consequences of compassion at work. *Journal of Organizational Behavior*, 29(2), 193–218. https://doi.org/10.1002/job.508

18. Owens, B. P., & Hekman, D. R. (2012). Modeling how to grow: An inductive examination of humble leader behaviors, contingencies, and outcomes. *Academy of Management Journal*, 55(4), 787–818. https://doi.org/10.5465/amj.2010.0441

19. Porath, C., & Pearson, C. (2013). The price of incivility. *Harvard Business Review*, 91(1–2), 114–121. https://hbr.org/2013/01/the-price-of-incivility

20. Yam, K. C., Christian, M. S., Wei, W., Liao, Z., & Nai, J. (2017). The mixed blessing of leader sense of humor: Examining costs and benefits. *Academy of Management Journal*, 61(1), 348–369. https://doi.org/10.5465/amj.2016.0944

CHAPTER 5: THE TRANSFORMATIONAL POWER OF COMPETITIVE KINDNESS ON INDIVIDUALS AND ORGANIZATIONS

21. Lutz, A., Slagter, H. A., Dunne, J. D., & Davidson, R. J. (2004). Attention regulation and monitoring in meditation. *Trends in Cognitive Sciences*, 8(4), 163-169.

22. Seppälä, E. M., Rossomando, T., & Doty, J. R. (2017). Social connection and compassion: Important predictors of health and well-being. *Social Research*, 80(2), 411-430.

23. Porges, S. W. (2011). *The Polyvagal Theory: Neurophysiological foundations of emotions, attachment, communication, and self-regulation*. W. W. Norton & Company.

24. Jazaieri, H., Jinpa, G. T., McGonigal, K., Rosenberg, E. L., Finkelstein, J., Simon-Thomas, E., ... & Goldin, P. R. (2013). Enhancing compassion: A randomized controlled trial of a compassion cultivation training program. *Journal of Happiness Studies*, 14(4), 1113-1126.

25. Rozovsky, J. (2015). The five keys to a successful Google team. *Google re: Work*. Retrieved from https://rework.withgoogle.com/blog/five-keys-to-a-successful-google-team/

26. Edmondson, A. C. (2019). *The Fearless Organization: Creating psychological safety in the workplace for learning, innovation, and growth*. John Wiley & Sons.

27. Catalyst. (2020). *The Power of Inclusive Leadership*. Retrieved from https://www.catalyst.org/research/inclusive-leadership-report/

28. McKinsey & Company. (2020). *Diversity wins: How inclusion matters*. Retrieved from https://www.mckinsey.com/featured-insights/diversity-and-inclusion/diversity-wins-how-inclusion-matters

29. Goleman, D., Boyatzis, R., & McKee, A. (2013). *Primal Leadership: Realizing the power of emotional intelligence*. Harvard Business Review Press.

30. Southwick, S. M., & Charney, D. S. (2012). *Resilience: The science of mastering life's greatest challenges*. Cambridge University Press.

31. Gallup. (2023). *State of the Global Workplace 2023*. Retrieved from https://www.gallup.com/workplace/349484/state-of-the-global-workplace.aspx

32. Liu, W., Tangirala, S., Lam, W., Chen, Z., Jia, R. T., & Huang, X. (2018). How and when peers' positive mood influences employees' voice. *Journal of Applied Psychology, 103*(8), 823-837.

33. Van Velsor, E., McCauley, C. D., & Ruderman, M. N. (2010). *The Center for Creative Leadership handbook of leadership development* (3rd ed.). Jossey-Bass.

34. Frost, P. J. (2003). *Toxic emotions at work: How compassionate managers handle pain and conflict.* Harvard Business Review Press.

35. Grant, A. M. (2013). *Give and Take: Why helping others drives our success.* Viking Press.

36. George, B. (2003). *Authentic Leadership: Rediscovering the secrets to creating lasting value.* Jossey-Bass.

37. Dutton, J. E., Workman, K. M., & Hardin, A. E. (2006). Compassion at work. *Annual Review of Organizational Psychology and Organizational Behavior, 1,* 277-304.

38. McCauley, C. D., Van Velsor, E., & Ruderman, M. N. (2010). *The Center for Creative Leadership handbook of leadership development* (3rd ed.). Jossey-Bass.

CHAPTER 6: COMPETITIVE KINDNESS VS. COMPETITIVE CRUELTY

39. Greenleaf, R. K. (1977). *Servant leadership: A journey into the nature of legitimate power and greatness.*

40. Kets de Vries, M. F. R. (2006). *The leadership mystique: Leading behavior in the human enterprise.*

41. Edmondson, A. (1999). Psychological safety and learning behavior in work teams. *Administrative Science Quarterly, 44*(2), 350-383.

42. Lilius, J. M., Worline, M. C., Maitlis, S., Kanov, J., Dutton, J. E., & Frost, P. (2008). The contours and consequences of compassion at work. *Journal of Organizational Behavior, 29*(2), 193-218.

43. Maslach, C., & Leiter, M. P. (2016). *Burnout: A multidimensional perspective.* Taylor & Francis.

44. Dutton, J. E., Workman, K. M., & Hardin, A. E. (2014). Compassion at work. *Annual Review of Organizational Psychology and Organizational Behavior, 1*(1), 277-304.

45. Hogan, R., & Kaiser, R. B. (2005). What we know about leadership. *Review of General Psychology, 9*(2), 169-180.

46. Gallup. (2023). *State of the Global Workplace 2023 Report.*

47. Sutton, R. I. (2007). *The No Asshole Rule: Building a Civilized Workplace and Surviving One That Isn't.* Warner Business Books.

48. Detert, J. R., & Edmondson, A. C. (2011). Implicit voice theories: Taken-for-granted rules of self-censorship at work. *Academy of Management Journal, 54*(3), 461-488.

49. Kelloway, E. K., Sivanathan, N., Francis, L., & Barling, J. (2005). Poor leadership and workplace safety. *Journal of Occupational Health Psychology, 10*(1), 11.

50. Seppälä, E., Rossomando, T., & Doty, J. R. (2017). Social connection and compassion: Important predictors of health and well-being. *Social Research, 80*(2), 411-430.

51. Cameron, K. S. (2011). *Positive leadership: Strategies for extraordinary performance*. Berrett-Koehler Publishers.

52. Ashkanasy, N. M., & Humphrey, R. H. (2011). A multi-level view of leadership and emotions. *The Leadership Quarterly, 22*(6), 1032-1044.

CHAPTER 8: UNSHAKABLE INTEGRITY

53. Jones, R. T., & Keeler, O. B. (1960). *Golf Is My Game*. Doubleday.

54. Hesselbein, F. (2002). *Hesselbein on Leadership*. Jossey-Bass.

55. Buffett, W. (2013). Letter to Berkshire Hathaway Shareholders. Berkshire Hathaway Inc.

56. Center for Creative Leadership. (2019). "Integrity and Leadership Effectiveness: A Longitudinal Study." *Leadership Quarterly, 30*(4), 445-462.

57. Kouzes, J. M., & Posner, B. Z. (2017). *The Leadership Challenge: How to Make Extraordinary Things Happen in Organizations* (6th ed.). Jossey-Bass.

58. Zak, P. J. (2017). "The Neuroscience of Trust." *Harvard Business Review, 95*(1), 84-90.

59. Covey, S. R. (1989). *The 7 Habits of Highly Effective People*. Free Press.

60. Schwartz, B. (2004). "The Paradox of Choice and Decision-Making Research." *Journal of Consumer Psychology, 14*(3), 332-336.

61. Cialdini, R. B. (2006). *Influence: The Psychology of Persuasion*. Harper Business.

62. Angelou, M. (1969). *I Know Why the Caged Bird Sings*. Random House.

63. Duhigg, C. (2016). "What Google Learned From Its Quest to Build the Perfect Team." *The New York Times Magazine*.

64. Einstein, A. (1955). *Ideas and Opinions*. Crown Publishers.

65. Kaptein, M. (2008). "Developing and Testing a Measure for the Ethical Culture of Organizations." *Journal of Business Ethics, 78*(4), 635-649.

66. Haidt, J. (2003). "Elevation and the Positive Psychology of Morality." *Flourishing: Positive Psychology and the Life Well-Lived*, 275-289.

CHAPTER 9: GENUINE AUTHENTICITY

67. Walumbwa, F. O., Avolio, B. J., Gardner, W. L., Wernsing, T. S., & Peterson, S. J. (2008). Authentic leadership: Development and validation of a theory-based measure. *Journal of Management, 34*(1), 89-126.

68. Zak, P. J. (2017). *Trust factor: The science of creating high-performance companies*. AMACOM.

69. Rock, D. (2008). SCARF: A brain-based model for collaborating with and influencing others. *NeuroLeadership Journal, 1*(1), 44-52.

70. George, B. (2003). *Authentic leadership: Rediscovering the secrets to creating lasting value* (p. 12). Jossey-Bass.

71. Gallup. (2023). *State of the global workplace*. Gallup Press.

72. Avolio, B. J., & Gardner, W. L. (2005). Authentic leadership development: Getting to the root of positive forms of leadership. *The Leadership Quarterly, 16*(3), 315-338.

73. Brown, B. (2018). *Dare to lead: Brave work, tough conversations, whole hearts*. Random House.

74. Brown, B. (2018). *Dare to lead: Brave work, tough conversations, whole hearts* (p. 19). Random House.

75. Grant, A. (2013). *Give and take: Why helping others drives our success.* Penguin Books.

76. Dweck, C. (2006). *Mindset: The new psychology of success.* Random House.

77. Collins, J. (2001). *Good to great: Why some companies make the leap... and others don't* (p. 33). HarperBusiness.

78. Edmondson, A. C. (2018). *The fearless organization: Creating psychological safety for learning, innovation, and growth.* Wiley.

CHAPTER 10: THE HUMBLE CHAMPION

79. Owens, B. P., Johnson, M. D., & Mitchell, T. R. (2013). Expressed humility in organizations: Implications for performance, teams, and leadership. *Organization Science,* 24(5), 1517-1538.

80. Holiday, R. (2016). *Ego is the enemy.* Portfolio.

81. Gibb, J. R. (1961). Defensive communication. *Journal of Communication,* 11(3), 141-148.

82. Rock, D. (2008). SCARF: A brain-based model for collaborating with and influencing others. *NeuroLeadership Journal,* 1(1), 44-52.

83. Kern, M. L., et al. (2020). The neurological foundations of humble leadership: Executive function and emotional regulation in leadership effectiveness. *Journal of Applied Psychology,* 105(8), 847-865.

84. Owens, B. P., & Hekman, D. R. (2012). Modeling how to grow: An inductive examination of humble leader behaviors, contingencies, and outcomes. *Academy of Management Journal,* 55(4), 787-818.

85. Grant, A. (2013). *Give and take: A revolutionary approach to success.* Viking.

86. Dweck, C. S. (2006). *Mindset: The new psychology of success.* Random House.

87. Worline, M. C., & Dutton, J. E. (2017). *Awakening compassion at work: The quiet power that elevates people and organizations.* Berrett-Koehler Publishers.

88. Frei, F., & Morriss, A. (2020). *Unleashed: The unapologetic leader's guide to empowering everyone around you.* Harvard Business Review Press.

89. Collins, J. (2001). *Good to great: Why some companies make the leap... and others don't.* HarperBusiness.

90. Quote attributed to Maya Angelou, though specific source varies across collections of her wisdom.

91. Edmondson, A. (2019). *The fearless organization: Creating psychological safety in the workplace for learning, innovation, and growth.* Wiley.

92. Grant, A. (2016). Originals: How non-conformists move the world. *Academy of Management Perspectives,* 30(1), 96-98.

93. *Tao Te Ching,* Chapter 63. Translation varies by interpreter; this reflects the essence found in most scholarly translations.

CHAPTER 11: VISION-DRIVEN ENCOURAGER

94. Gallup. (2020). *State of the Global Workplace Report.*

95. Harvard Business Review. (2019). "The Business Case for Purpose-Driven Leadership."

96. University of Rochester. (2021). "Goal Visualization and Achievement Outcomes."

97. Lopez, S. J. (2013). *Making Hope Happen: Create the Future You Want.* Atria Books.

98. MIT Sloan Management Review. (2020). "Vision Communication and Organizational Performance."

99. Deloitte. (2020). *The Social Enterprise at Work: Purpose-Driven Leadership.*

100. University of Pennsylvania. (2019). "Recognition, Performance, and Retention Study."

101. University of Michigan. (2018). "Optimistic Leadership and Team Performance."

102. Gallup. (2021). *Manager Engagement and Business Outcomes.*

103. Cameron, K. S. (2012). *Positive Leadership: Strategies for Extraordinary Performance.* Berrett-Koehler.

104. University of Kansas. (2019). "Hope, Employee Engagement, and Workplace Performance."

105. Snyder, C. R. (2002). "Hope Theory: Rainbows in the Mind." *Psychological Inquiry,* 13(4), 249-275.

106. Harvard Medical School. (2021). "Gratitude and Hope: Neural Pathways to Well-being."

107. University of Pennsylvania. (2020). "Leadership Hope and Team Performance Outcomes."

CHAPTER 12: EMPOWER INDIVIDUAL WORTH

108. Herrmann, N. (1996). *The Whole Brain Business Book: Unlocking the Power of Whole Brain Thinking in Organizations and Individuals.* McGraw-Hill Professional.

109. Page, S. E. (2017). *The Diversity Bonus: How Great Teams Pay Off.* Princeton University Press.

110. Taylor, A. R. (2008). *Realizing My Potential.* AuthorHouse.

111. Edmondson, A. C. (2019). *The Fearless Organization: Creating Psychological Safety for Learning, Innovation, and Growth.* Wiley.

112. Bunderson, J. S., & Sutcliffe, K. M. (2002). Comparing alternative conceptualizations of functional diversity in management teams: Process and performance effects. *Academy of Management Journal,* 45(5), 875-893.

CHAPTER 13: ELEVATE OTHERS THROUGH SERVICE

113. Herrmann, N. (1996). *The Whole Brain Business Book: Unlocking the Power of Whole Brain Thinking in Organizations and Individuals.* McGraw-Hill Professional.

114. Page, S. E. (2017). *The Diversity Bonus: How Great Teams Pay Off.* Princeton University Press.

115. Taylor, A. R. (2008). *Realizing My Potential.* AuthorHouse.

116. Edmondson, A. C. (2019). *The Fearless Organization: Creating Psychological Safety for Learning, Innovation, and Growth.* Wiley.

117. Bunderson, J. S., & Sutcliffe, K. M. (2002). Comparing alternative conceptualizations of functional diversity in management teams: Process and performance effects. *Academy of Management Journal,* 45(5), 875-893.

118. Hu, D., Thien, L. M., Ahmi, A., & Mohamed, A. (2023). The 100 most-cited research publications on servant leadership: A bibliometric analysis. *SAGE Open,* 13(3).

119. Cooley, C. H. (1902). *Human nature and the social order.* Charles Scribner's Sons.

120. Mead, G. H. (1934). *Mind, self, and society.* University of Chicago Press.

121. Rosenthal, R., & Jacobson, L. (1968). Pygmalion in the classroom. *The Urban Review,* 3(1), 16-20.

122. Izuma, K., Saito, D. N., & Sadato, N. (2008). Processing of social and monetary rewards in the human striatum. *Neuron,* 58(2), 284-294.

123. Rock, D. (2008). SCARF: A brain-based model for collaborating with and influencing others. *NeuroLeadership Journal,* 1(1), 44-52.

124. Clifton, D. O., & Harter, J. K. (2003). Investing in strengths. In K. S. Cameron, J. E. Dutton, & R. E. Quinn (Eds.), *Positive organizational scholarship* (pp. 111-121). Berrett-Koehler Publishers.

125. Bass, B. M., & Riggio, R. E. (2006). *Transformational leadership* (2nd ed.). Lawrence Erlbaum Associates.

126. Tajfel, H., & Turner, J. C. (1979). An integrative theory of intergroup conflict. In W. G. Austin & S. Worchel (Eds.), *The social psychology of intergroup relations* (pp. 33-47). Brooks/Cole.

127. Dutton, J. E., Roberts, L. M., & Bednar, J. (2010). Pathways for positive identity construction at work. *Academy of Management Review,* 35(2), 265-293.

128. Schein, E. H. (2010). *Organizational culture and leadership* (4th ed.). Jossey-Bass.

129. Goleman, D. (2000). Leadership that gets results. *Harvard Business Review,* 78(2), 78-90.

130. Avolio, B. J., & Gardner, W. L. (2005). Authentic leadership development. *The Leadership Quarterly,* 16(3), 315-338.

131. Buckingham, M., & Coffman, C. (1999). *First, break all the rules.* Simon & Schuster.

132. Dweck, C. S. (2006). Mindset: The new psychology of success. Random House.

133. Markus, H., & Nurius, P. (1986). Possible selves. *American Psychologist,* 41(9), 954-969.

134. Weiner, B. (1985). An attributional theory of achievement motivation and emotion. *Psychological Review,* 92(4), 548-573.

135. Kluger, A. N., & DeNisi, A. (1996). The effects of feedback interventions on performance. *Psychological Bulletin,* 119(2), 254-284.

136. Losada, M., & Heaphy, E. (2004). The role of positivity and connectivity in the performance of business teams. *American Behavioral Scientist,* 47(6), 740-765.

137. Corporate Leadership Council. (2008). *Performance management survey.* Corporate Executive Board.

138. Edmondson, A. (1999). Psychological safety and learning behavior in work teams. *Administrative Science Quarterly,* 44(2), 350-383.

139. Duhigg, C. (2016). What Google learned from its quest to build the perfect team. *The New York Times Magazine,* February 25, 2016.

140. Barsade, S. G. (2002). The ripple effect: Emotional contagion and its influence on group behavior. *Administrative Science Quarterly,* 47(4), 644-675.

141. Brackett, M. A., Rivers, S. E., & Salovey, P. (2011). Emotional intelligence: Implications for personal, social, academic, and workplace success. *Social and Personality Psychology Compass,* 5(1), 88-103.

142. Mehrabian, A. (1971). *Silent messages.* Wadsworth Publishing.

143. Blau, P. M. (1964). *Exchange and power in social life.* John Wiley & Sons.

144. Zenger, J., & Folkman, J. (2009). *The extraordinary leader: Turning good managers into great leaders*. McGraw-Hill.

145. Cooperrider, D. L., & Whitney, D. (2005). *Appreciative inquiry: A positive revolution in change*. Berrett-Koehler Publishers.

146. Cameron, K. S. (2012). *Positive leadership: Strategies for extraordinary performance*. Berrett-Koehler Publishers.

CHAPTER 15: PURSUE EXCELLENCE WITH COMPASSION

147. Boyle, G. (2017). *Barking to the Choir: The Power of Radical Kinship*. Simon & Schuster.

148. Aboobaker, N., Edward, M., & Zulkifli, F. (2023). Whither compassionate leadership? A systematic review. *Management Review Quarterly*, 73(3), 1157-1195.

149. Strauss, C., Taylor, B. L., Gu, J., Kuyken, W., Baer, R., Jones, F., & Cavanagh, K. (2016). What is compassion and how can we measure it? A review of definitions and measures. *Clinical Psychology Review*, 47, 15-27.

150. Goetz, J. L., Keltner, D., & Simon-Thomas, E. (2010). Compassion: An evolutionary analysis and empirical review. *Psychological Bulletin*, 136(3), 351-374.

151. Kanov, J. M., Maitlis, S., Worline, M. C., Dutton, J. E., Frost, P. J., & Lilius, J. M. (2004). Compassion in organizational life. *American Behavioral Scientist*, 47(6), 808-827.

152. Duhigg, C. (2016). What Google learned from its quest to build the perfect team. *The New York Times Magazine*, February 25, 2016.

153. Zenger, J., & Folkman, J. (2019). The ideal praise-to-criticism ratio. *Harvard Business Review*, March 15, 2019.

154. Boyatzis, R., Smith, M., & Beveridge, A. (2013). Coaching with compassion: Inspiring health, well-being, and development in organizations. *The Journal of Applied Behavioral Science*, 49(2), 153-178.

155. Trzeciak, S., & Mazzarelli, A. (2019). *Compassionomics: The Revolutionary Scientific Evidence That Caring Makes a Difference*. Studer Group.

156. Worline, M. C., & Dutton, J. E. (2017). *Awakening Compassion at Work: The Quiet Power That Elevates People and Organizations*. Berrett-Koehler Publishers.

CHAPTER 16: WHAT TO DO
WHEN BEING KIND FEELS IMPOSSIBLE OR UNNATURAL

157. Kight, T. (2018). *Focus 3: E+R=O - The Foundation of Mental Toughness*. Focus 3 Leadership. https://focus3.com/e-r-o/

158. Kight, T. (2019). *Above the Line: Lessons in Leadership and Life from a Championship Program*. McGraw-Hill Education.

159. Brown, B. (2018). *Dare to Lead: Brave Work, Tough Conversations, Whole Hearts*. Random House.

160. Ueshiba, M. (1991). *The Art of Peace*. Translated by John Stevens. Shambhala Publications.

161. Meyer, U. (2015). *Above the Line: Lessons in Leadership and Life from a Championship Program*. Penguin Press. (Source for the 6 R Factor disciplines)

ABOUT THE AUTHOR

 Dr. Rob Clark is a senior executive in intercollegiate athletics with over twenty years of experience leading high-performing organizations throughout the United States. His teams have generated hundreds of millions in revenue and supported numerous conference and national champions.

He earned a PhD from Texas A&M and holds a master's degree and bachelor's degree from Occidental College. He has published scholarly research on institutional ethics, culture, and organizational effectiveness. A fourth-generation college athlete, he served as team captain of his nationally ranked football team and continues to serve members of the community through voluntary ecclesiastical service.

He resides in Utah with his wife, Emily, and their children Annie, Kate, and McCoy.

Representing a community of authors whose books have collectively sold hundreds of millions of copies, the founders of The Gray + Miller Agency launched Maison Vero, a professional publishing house that partners with rising authors to bring their thought leadership to the world. Our representation covers every aspect of thought leadership, including U.S. senators, governors, and ambassadors, billionaire founders and entrepreneurs, researchers, academics, scientists, consultants, practitioners, social influencers, C-suite leaders, adventurers, professional athletes, artists, and creators. We partner with thought leaders and world changers like you who have a story to tell. By bringing decades of professional expertise to our clients, we are charting a new path in a timeless industry that transcends publishing norms, transforming powerful thoughts into impactful books that inspire minds, ignite hearts, and open doors.

Visit maisonvero.com to view our growing list of authors, or to submit a proposal for publication consideration.

Follow Maison Vero for insight and inspiration on social media:

 MaisonVero  MaisonVero  MaisonVeroPublishing

For information about special discounts for bulk purchases, please call (949) 333-4872 or email info@graymilleragency.com.

Maison Vero is a partner brand of The Gray + Miller Agency, a speaking, literary, and talent consortium. For more information on the talent represented by The Gray + Miller Agency, or to bring any of our thought leaders to your organization or live event, please visit our website at **graymilleragency.com**.

www.ingramcontent.com/pod-product-compliance
Lightning Source LLC
Chambersburg PA
CBHW021126070726

47591CB00014B/1678